Edexcel GCSE
Religious Studies

Unit 3
Religion and Life
Roman Catholic Christianity

Angela Hylton
Lesley Seery

Published by Pearson Education Limited, a company incorporated in England and Wales, having its registered office at Edinburgh Gate, Harlow, Essex, CM20 2JE. Registered company number: 872828

www.pearsonschoolsandfecolleges.co.uk

Edexcel is a registered trade mark of Edexcel Limited

Text © Pearson Education Ltd 2009
First published 2009

14
10 9 8 7 6 5 4

British Library Cataloguing in Publication Data
A catalogue record for this book is available from the British Library.
ISBN 978 1 846904 21 9

Produced and Edited by Florence Production Ltd, Stoodleigh, Devon
Typeset and illustrated by HL Studios, Long Hanborough, Oxford
Original illustrations © Pearson Education Ltd 2009
Cover design by Pearson Education Ltd
Picture research by Zooid
Cover photo/illustration © Igor Sinitsyn/Alamy
Printed in Malaysia, (CTP-VVP)

Acknowledgements
The authors and publisher would like to thank the following individuals and organisations for permission to reproduce copyright material:

Abortion Rights, p. 39; Alberto E. Rodriguez/Getty Images, p. 68; Alison Quince/CAFOD, p. 49; Anatomical Travelogue/Science Photo Library, p. 38; Anjum Naveed/Associated Press/PA Photos, p. 89; Antix Productions, p. 32; Anwar Hussein/allaction.co.uk/PA Photos, p. 57; Associated Press/Press Association Images, p. 85; BBC Photograph Library, p. 57; BBC/Tiger Aspect Productions, p. 106; Bettmann/Corbis UK Ltd., p. 15; Brownstock Inc./Alamy, p. 67; c.20thC.Fox/Everett/Rex Features, pp. 78, 106; c.Newmarket/Everett/Rex Features, p. 90; CAFOD, p. 49; Caters News Agency Ltd/Rex Features, p. 43; Charles Thatcher/Getty Images, p. 74; China Photos/Getty Images, p. 19; Classic Image/Alamy, p. 86; ClassicStock/Alamy, p. 86; Craig Hibbert/Solo Syndication, p. 37; Daniel Hambury/Epa/Corbis UK Ltd., p. 69; EMPICS Sports Photo Agency/PA Photos, p. 85; Franco Origlia/Getty Images, p. 98; Getty Images, p. 43; Hammondovi/iStockphoto, p. 60; Henryk T Kaiser/age fotostock/Photolibrary Group, p. 10; Hulton-Deutsch Collection/Corbis UK Ltd., pp. 86, 92; Ian Waldie/Reuters/Corbis UK Ltd., p. 86; ITV/Rex Features, p. 106; Jacques deLacroix/Alamy, p. 64; Jason Friend Photography Ltd/Alamy, p. 105; Jim West/Alamy, p. 3; John Lund/Corbis UK Ltd., p. 3; Kes/www.CartoonStock.com, p. 63; Kevin Carter/Megan Patricia Carter Trust/Sygma/Corbis UK Ltd., p. 46; Lime Pictures Publicity, p. 51; Look and Learn/Bridgeman Art Library, p. 57; Lorelyn Medina/Shutterstock, p. 14; Louvre/Bridgeman Art Library, p. 17; lxd/Shutterstock, p. 8; M.T.M. Images/Alamy, p. 72; Mahmud Hams/AFP/Getty Images, p. 16; Mark Renders/Getty Images, p. 97; Markus Moellenberg/Zefa/Corbis UK Ltd., p. 57; Micah Ian Wright & AntiWarPosters.com, p. 107; Ousama Ayoub/AFP/Getty Images, p. 104; PA Photos, p. 86; PA WIRE/PA Photos, p. 44; Peter Barritt/Alamy, p. 3; ProLife Alliance, p. 39; Revolution Studios and Columbia/album/akg-images, p. 59; Ronald Grant Archive, p. 22; Salvatore Laporta/Getty Images, p. 105; The Scout Association, p. 72; Shaun Curry/AFP/Getty Images, p. 51; The Bridgeman Art Library/Getty Images, p. 86; Tim Graham/Getty Images, p. 86; Toby Melville/Reuters/Corbis UK Ltd., p. 89; Tracy Whiteside/Shutterstock, p. 60; Universal Pictures/Album/akg-images, p. 3; Victor Burnside/Shutterstock, 9; Vivid Pixels/Shutterstock, p. 4; WMAP Science Team, NASA/Science Photo Library, p. 13; www.art4us.me.uk, p. 35; Yuri Arcurs/Shutterstock, p. 86.

Permissions acknowledgements
Scripture taken from the Holy Bible, New International Version®. Copyright © 1973, 1978, 1984 International Bible Society. Used by permission of Zondervan. All rights reserved.

UK Census 2001, Crown copyright, reproduced under the terms of the Click-Use Licence, p. 27; Catechism of the Catholic Church, reproduced by kind permission of Continuum International Publishing Group, pp. 31, 62, 101; Dr Sam Parnia quoted in 'Study into near death experiences' by Jane Dreaper, University of Southampton, from BBC News, 18 September 2008, p. 33; Matt Hampson quoted in 'Why Matt Hampson chose to live', the Sunday Times 19 October 2008, http://www.timesonline.co.uk/tol/news/uk/article4969444.ece, p.43; J. Reynolds and P. Mansfield, 'The Effect of Changing Attitudes to Marriage on its Stability', Lord Chancellor's Department Research Series, No. 2/1999, reproduced under the terms of the Click-Use Licence, p. 60; Definitions found in http://www.brook.org.uk/content/, pp. 74, 75; Economic & Social Research Council, 'Ethnic Minorities in the UK' http://www.esrcsocietytoday.ac.uk/ESRCInfoCentre/facts/index39.aspx?ComponentId=12534&SourcePageId=12705, p. 92; The Independent Television Commission report quoted in http://news.bbc.co.uk/1/hi/entertainment/1394364.stm, p. 107; Sir Ian Blair, quoted in 'Met chief accuses media of racism', BBC News, 26 January 2006, http://news.bbc.co.uk/1/hi/england/london/4651368.stm, p. 107.

Every effort has been made to contact copyright holders of material reproduced in this book. Any omissions will be rectified in subsequent printings if notice is given to the publishers.

Websites
There are links to relevant websites in this book. In order to ensure that the links are up to date, that the links work, and that the sites are not inadvertently linked to sites that could be considered offensive, we have made the links available on the Heinemann website at www.heinemann.co.uk/hotlinks. When you access the site, the express code is 4219P.

Disclaimer
This material has been published on behalf of Edexcel and offers high-quality support for the delivery of Edexcel qualifications.
This does not mean that the material is essential to achieve any Edexcel qualification, nor does it mean that it is the only suitable material available to support any Edexcel qualification. Edexcel material will not be used verbatim in setting any Edexcel examination or assessment. Any resource lists produced by Edexcel shall include this and other appropriate resources.

Copies of official specifications for all Edexcel qualifications may be found on the Edexcel website: www.edexcel.com

Contents

Welcome to this Edexcel GCSE in Religious Studies Resource

These resources have been written to support fully Edexcel's new specification for GCSE Religious Studies. Each student book covers one unit of the specification which makes up a Short Course qualification. Any two units from separate modules of the specification make up a Full Course qualification. Written by experienced examiners and packed with exam tips and activities, these books include lots of engaging features to enthuse students and provide the range of support needed to make teaching and learning a success for all ability levels.

Features in this book

In each section you will find the following features:

- **an introductory spread** which introduces the topics and gives the Edexcel key terms and learning outcomes for the whole section

- **topic spreads** containing the following features:

  - **Learning outcomes** for the topic

  - edexcel ⠿ key terms

    Specification key terms – are emboldened and defined for easy reference

  - ### Glossary

    Here we define other complex terms to help with understanding

  - **Activities** and **For discussion** panels provide stimulating tasks for the classroom and homework
  - a topic **Summary** captures the main learning points.

How to use this book

This book supports Module A, Unit 3 Religion and Life, based on a study of Roman Catholic Christianity.

This book is split into the four sections of the specification.

A dedicated suite of revision resources for complete exam success. We've broken down the six stages of revision to ensure that you are prepared every step of the way.

How to get into the perfect 'zone' for your revision.

Tips and advice on how to effectively plan your revision.

Revision activities and exam-style practice at the end of every section plus additional exam practice at the end of the book.

Last-minute advice for just before the exam.

An overview of what you will have to do in the exam, plus a chance to see what a real exam paper will look like.

What do you do after your exam? This section contains information on how to get your results and answers to frequently asked questions on what to do next.

ResultsPlus

These features are based on how students have performed in past exams. They are combined with expert advice and guidance from examiners to show you how to achieve better results.

There are five different types of ResultsPlus features throughout this book:

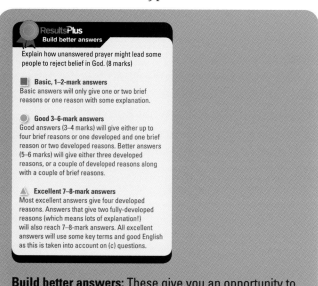

Build better answers: These give you an opportunity to answer some exam-style questions. They contain tips for what a basic ■ good ○ and excellent △ answer will contain.

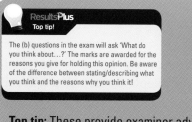

Top tip: These provide examiner advice and guidance to help improve your results.

Watch out! These warn you about common mistakes and misconceptions that examiners frequently see students make. Make sure that you don't repeat them!

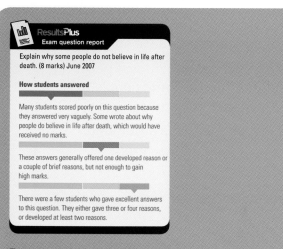

Exam question report: These show previous exam questions with details about how well students answered them.

Red shows the number of students who scored low marks (less than 35% of the total marks).

Orange shows the number of students who did okay (scoring between 35% and 70% of the total marks).

Green shows the number of students who did well (scoring over 70% of the total marks).

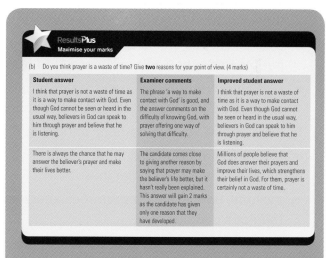

Maximise your marks: These are featured in the KnowZone (see 'How to use this book' on previous page) at the end of each chapter. They include an exam-style question with a student answer, examiner comments and an improved answer so that you can see how to build a better response.

Believing in God

Introduction

In this section you will consider why Roman Catholics and other Christians do believe in God and why other people do not. You will reflect on your own thoughts about God and what reasons and evidence you have for this viewpoint. You will learn what Roman Catholics believe about God and about the many ways (reasons and evidence) they come to this decision. You will also learn about the things that challenge Christian beliefs about God and how they respond to these challenges.

Learning outcomes for this section

By the end of this section you should be able to:

- give definitions of the key terms
- outline or describe the features of a Roman Catholic upbringing and how it may lead to belief in God
- explain how people come to believe in God through having a religious experience
- outline or describe different explanations of the origins of the universe, including the 'causation', 'design' and scientific arguments
- explain why scientific explanations of the origins of the universe cause some people to doubt God's existence, and how Christians respond to this
- outline or describe other examples of problems that may cause some people to doubt God's existence; for example, unanswered prayers or evil and suffering
- explain how Roman Catholic and other Christians respond to these arguments
- explain, with examples, how media programmes about religion may affect a person's attitude to belief in God
- evaluate why these programmes affect people's beliefs and whether this is fair to religious people
- express with reasons and evidence your own opinion about the reasons for believing or not believing in God, and your own thoughts about whether God exists.

---

edexcel ::: key terms

agnosticism	free will	natural evil	omnipotent
atheism	miracle	numinous	omniscient
conversion	moral evil	omni-benevolent	prayer

Fascinating fact

According to surveys in the UK, around 70 per cent of people claim to believe in some sort of God.

Look at the pictures – each one is a picture of what someone thinks God is like.

- Which is the odd one out?
- Which is closest to your idea about God? Why?
- Each picture raises some questions about God. What questions do you think they raise?

1.1 Catholic upbringing and belief in God

Learning outcomes

By the end of this lesson you should be able to:

- describe a Roman Catholic upbringing
- explain how a Roman Catholic upbringing may lead to or support belief in God
- give examples from your own upbringing of things that have influenced you.

Glossary

Baptism – Rite of initiation involving immersion in, or sprinkling or pouring of, water.

Confirmation – Confirming your baptismal vows for yourself and receiving the Holy Spirit.

First Holy Communion – Receiving the body and blood of Jesus for the first time.

Reconciliation (confession) – Repairing your relationship with God and the community.

Sacrament – Outward sign of something holy, it usually is representative of some part of God's relationship with human beings, e.g. baptism or Eucharist.

Parents are the ones who make most of the day-to-day decisions in their young children's lives. They choose what clothes they should wear, what food they should eat and so on. Many parents feel that something as important as their religion should also not be ignored and so they choose to raise their children within their own faith.

Catholic parents will ensure that their baby is baptised. The parents and the godparents make promises that they will raise the baby as a Catholic. It is their duty to carry out these promises as the child grows.

Catholic children are taken to Mass each Sunday and encouraged to take an active part in it. They may also attend Sunday school to learn more about their faith.

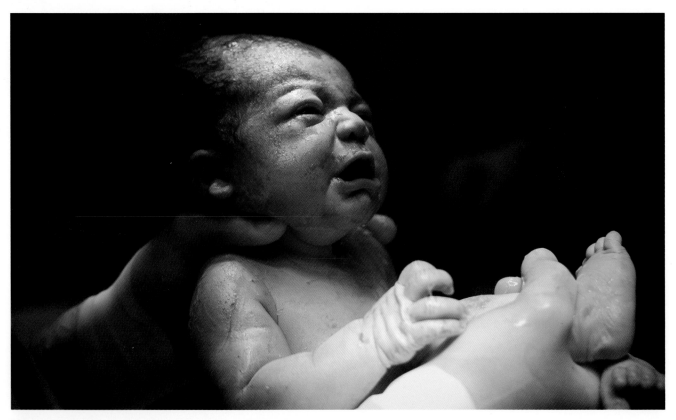

What can parents do for this baby to ensure that he/she is raised as a Roman Catholic?

At home, parents are the first 'teachers' of their children. Catholic parents teach their children to make the sign of the cross and say simple prayers, often at bedtime. Children are taught to say thank you to God, too, for all the things that they have. Each child may own a children's Bible (often given to them at baptism) from which to learn simple Bible stories. They will also celebrate all the main festivals at home with their parents, who will teach them the meaning of each festival as it occurs. Parents have a duty to set a good Catholic example to their children in the way that they interact with others and with the rest of the community. The children can then learn from them and copy their example.

Many Catholic parents will also ensure that their children attend a Catholic primary and secondary school. At school, the pupils will take part in different activities that will teach them about their faith. These include assemblies, special school Masses and religious studies lessons that focus on the Catholic faith. Perhaps one of the most important aspects of such a school is the Catholic atmosphere that exists there. The rules of the school will usually be based within the teachings of the Roman Catholic faith, and the majority of the pupils there will also be Catholic.

Catholic children are likely to learn about the sacraments both at home and at school. Their first Holy Communion will be a very special time. Children are also encouraged to attend reconciliation regularly (a sacrament in which they are forgiven for their sins) and to receive confirmation (a sacrament in which they confirm that they do want to be a Catholic) when they are old enough to do so.

Understanding the faith for themselves

By attending Mass each Sunday and on holy days, Catholic children can come to experience the presence of Christ during the Mass, and learn about the rite of the Mass. By attending with their families each week, children can learn how important the faith is to them and the need for a commitment to the faith. At Sunday school, they may also gain a deeper understanding of the Mass and the themes of the Mass. By becoming an altar server or a reader, children can begin to show their own commitment to the faith and provide a service to the community. In this way they are living out their own Catholic values.

Activities

2 Look at the main events that occur within a Catholic upbringing. How does each one help the child to have faith in God for themselves?

Challenge

3 Create a booklet about your own upbringing. You may want to include:

- photographs and information about your baptism or other ceremonies
- interviews with your parents or godparents or other family members about the way in which you were raised
- points about your school and the way in which this has affected your upbringing.

Activities

1 Design a timeline of a child's life, from the moment of birth until about the age of 16. Onto this timeline put events that would happen in the child's life that show he/she has a Roman Catholic upbringing. You can use the ideas that are included on this page, but also try to include more ideas of your own.

Summary

You now know the main features of a Roman Catholic upbringing and why some parents feel that it is important to raise their children in this way. You have learned about how this kind of upbringing would encourage belief in God.

1.2 Religious experience and belief in God

Learning outcomes

By the end of this lesson you should be able to:

- say what a religious experience is and give examples
- describe a religious experience
- explain why a religious experience may lead to or support belief in God.

Apart from a religious upbringing, there are four types of religious experience that people may encounter that can lead to a belief in God.

Numinous experience

A **numinous** experience is when something completely astonishes you. It is such an experience that words are not enough to describe the feeling, but it leaves you knowing that there must be something more powerful than you. Often, people refer to things in the natural world that are so beautiful they feel overwhelmed by them – for example, the view from a mountain top or a beautiful sunrise. For others, it may be an experience such as the birth of a baby. For some people this experience is so powerful that it convinces them that God must exist.

Conversion experience

There are two types of **conversion** experience. Some believers have conversion experiences during which their beliefs change from one faith to another, or from no faith to believing in God. The second type of conversion is when somebody decides that they want to devote themselves more entirely to their own faith.

Miracle

A **miracle** is when something happens that cannot be explained, and eventually people come to believe that God has made it happen. If a person witnesses an event that they believe God has caused or created, then their faith is likely to be strengthened.

edexcel ⠿ key terms

Conversion – When your life is changed by giving yourself to God.

Miracle – Something that seems to break a law of science and makes you think only God could have done it.

Numinous – The feeling of the presence of something greater than you.

Prayer – An attempt to contact God usually through words.

The Bible describes many miracles which Jesus performed. On one occasion it tells of how Jesus fed a crowd of 5,000 men with five loaves and two fish (Mark 6:30–44). How might the people present feel about God after witnessing this?

Prayer

If somebody prays to God they may feel that somebody is listening to them, and so believe that God is with them. This will help them to have faith in God. This experience can be even more powerful if the person feels that God has actually answered their **prayer**.

Activities

1 Draw and colour a spider diagram of the four different kinds of religious experience.

The numinous is very hard to explain. It is a feeling, and feelings sometimes can be very hard to put into words. It is for this reason that people often choose to express the numinous in terms of examples. A Roman Catholic example might be the experience of the presence of Christ during Mass.

St Paul had a conversion experience on the road to Damascus. He set off on his journey intending to persecute the early Christians. After seeing a blinding light and hearing a voice from Heaven, he completely changed and actually became a believer in Jesus himself. Most people do not experience such a dramatic change, but they do have a feeling that they must devote themselves more to their faith. For example, a person may perhaps stop going to Mass regularly. Then at some later point, they may have a conversion experience and begin to attend Mass regularly again and renew their faith.

There are two different kinds of miracles. The first is when something happens that someone can't explain scientifically and they begin to think that God must have made it happen. If this is the case, then a person's faith is increased. The second kind of miracle is called a *liberal miracle*. This is a kind of miracle that also requires some faith to begin with. For example, a baby may be born very prematurely and the parents are told that the baby will not survive, but against all the odds the baby does. Believing parents may choose to think that God has helped them, while the doctors may say that it was just the excellent care that was given to the baby.

A modern miracle at Lourdes

In October, 1987, 51 year-old Jean-Pierre Bely went on pilgrimage to Lourdes. He had been diagnosed with multiple sclerosis in the 1970s and by 1987 he was bound to a wheel chair and needed 24-hour care. On 8 October, Bely celebrated the Sacrament of Reconciliation and the next day he received the Sacrament of the Sick in the Rosary Square. Later that day, whilst lying in the sick room he experienced painful hot and cold sensations which grew very intense and he found that he could move his arms. That night, he woke up suddenly and was able to walk! He had regained the complete use of all his muscles and the medical scans no longer showed any trace of illness.

Activities

3 What is your reaction to the story of Jean-Pierre Bely? Do you believe that God cured him? How else would you explain what happened?

Challenge

4 Design and complete a survey about prayer. You might want to include questions such as *how often do people pray? what do they pray for?* and *do they feel that any of their prayers have been answered?* plus any other questions that you can think of. Analyse your survey – what conclusions can you draw from it?

Activities

2 Imagine that you have just experienced one of the four religious experiences. Write an account of your thoughts and feelings about what has just happened to you. Don't forget to include what you intend to do about this.

Summary

You have learned about four different kinds of religious experience, the numinous and conversion experiences, miracles and prayer. You should be able to explain how each of these would help somebody's faith in God to increase.

1.3 Belief in God – and the design argument

Learning outcomes

By the end of this lesson you should be able to:

● outline the design argument

● explain how the natural world might lead someone to belief in God, or support belief in God

● explain, with reasons and examples, your own opinion on the design argument.

The argument from design

(a) There is evidence of design in the world.
Many people say that the way that the universe is made suggests that it has been designed. For example, if the sun were slightly nearer or farther away from the Earth, then human life could not exist; it is in exactly the correct place. The human body is made up of many different parts that all seem to work perfectly with each other, and if they don't we begin to feel ill.

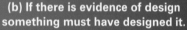

(b) If there is evidence of design something must have designed it.
Humans could not have created the universe so perfectly; we did not decide where to place the sun. We still do not know many things about the universe – if we did there would be no point in scientists doing research at all.

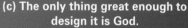

(c) The only thing great enough to design it is God.
As humans do not know exactly how the universe works, it must have been something that is much more intelligent than a human that has created the universe. The only thing this intelligent is God.

(d) Therefore God exists.
If God has designed the universe then God must exist.

Look closely at the picture of the sunflower. Why might some people believe that it looks like it has been designed?

The argument from design is sometimes also known as the *teleological* argument. The word teleological comes from the Greek word *telos*, which means 'end' or 'purpose'. The argument from design is often called the teleological argument as it assumes that there is a purpose within the world and nature.

Activities

1   Sum up the argument from design in just four sentences.

Paley's watch

William Paley was a great religious philosopher. In 1802 he wrote *Natural Theology*, in which he outlined the argument from design with an analogy of a watch. He said that if a person was walking along a beach and saw a stone, they wouldn't think much more about it. However, if a person was walking along a beach and saw a watch, they might take the watch home and take it apart. If they did so, they would assume – because a watch is so complex, with many different parts that all fit and work together – that somebody must have designed it. Paley went on to argue that the universe itself is so well designed, with many different parts that all fit and work so well together, that it too must have been designed. The only thing that is intelligent enough to do this is God. Therefore God must exist.

Would you be able to put the watch back together again? Would you be able to put a human body together so that it worked? Does this suggest design?

Activities

2   Imagine that you are a teacher of a Year 7 class and you have been asked to explain the argument from design to the class. What would you say?

3   If you could choose one thing that illustrated the argument from design, what would it be and why?

ResultsPlus
Build better answers

Do you think God designed the universe? Give **two** reasons for your point of view. (4 marks)

■   **Basic, 1-mark answers**
Students who receive low marks will give their own opinion but will not explain their reasons.

●   **Good, 2–3-mark answers**
These answers will either give two brief reasons for the student's opinion or one developed reason.

▲   **Excellent, 4-mark answers**
The best answers will offer two developed reasons for why the student does, or does not, believe that God designed the universe.

For discussion

Do you think that the argument from design 'proves' the existence of God? Why/why not?

Activities

Challenge

There are some criticisms of the argument from design. Some people argue that there is too big a jump to make from seeing patterns in nature to assuming that God must be responsible for these patterns. Others think that perhaps evolution was responsible for the perfect way in which nature seems to work.

4   Find out what David Hume or Thomas Aquinas said about the argument from design.

Summary

You should now know what the argument from design is, and be able to explain how William Paley linked this argument to finding a watch on a beach.

1.4 Causation and belief in God

Learning outcomes

By the end of this lesson you should be able to:

● outline reasons for believing in God based on the causation argument

● explain how the causation argument may or may not lead someone to believe in God

● express your own opinion about the strengths and weaknesses of this argument as reason or evidence for believing in God.

Activities

1 Can you think of something that has no cause?

In our world, there seems to be an accepted understanding that when something happens there must be something or someone who 'caused' it to happen. This allows us to blame people for the bad things that happen and celebrate the causes of good things that happen.

When it comes to the creation of the world and evidence that God exists, some people use similar arguments. They argue that nothing happens by chance – everything has a reason or a cause. This is known as *causation*.

The causation argument follows a logical route.

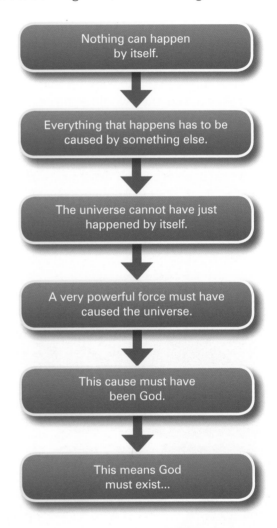

If we keep going back and back and back, we must come to the start of whatever started everything off. Some people say that the only thing powerful enough to start everything off would be God. Therefore, he has *caused* this to happen, and must exist.

A famous philosopher called Parmenides said that 'nothing comes from nothing'. In other words, everything must have been created by something else. This has led some people to believe that since the universe exists, it must have been created by something. Some people say that this something is God.

As each domino falls, it causes the next one in the line to fall, and so on. But what causes the first domino to fall?

Other people argue that this something was the 'big bang' (see pages 12–13). But then other people question who made the matter that collided to make the 'big bang' happen. For some people, the answer is always going to lead back to God.

We call this the 'first cause' (a cosmological argument) as it always leads back to God being the cause of the universe. If God is the 'first cause' of everything, then God must exist.

People's faith in God will be strengthened by this theory if it seems to them to be proof that God exists and that he has created the world.

ResultsPlus
Build better answers

Do you think God is the cause of the universe? Give **two** reasons for your opinion. (4 marks)

◼ **Basic, 1-mark answers**
In these answers the student will give their opinion but only supported by one basic reason.

● **Good, 2–3-mark answers**
Answers worth two marks will either give two basic reasons or one developed reason for their opinion. Three-mark answers will give one developed reason and one basic reason for their opinion.

▲ **Excellent, 4-mark answers**
The best answers will give two developed reasons for the student's opinion.

Activities

2 Examine this flow chart.

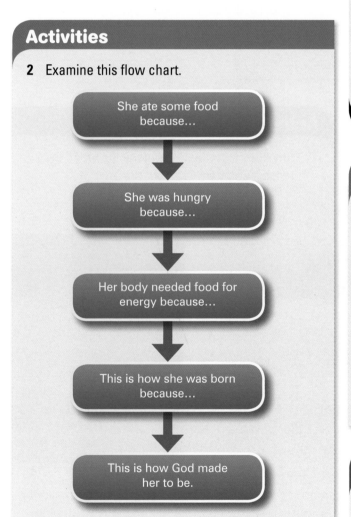

3 Can you produce your own five-step flow chart linking back to God?

Activities

4 Imagine that you have just been asked to prove that God exists – how would you do this using the causation argument?

Challenge

5 Research the works of Thomas Aquinas on the causation argument as a proof of God's existence.

6 Do you think that the causation argument has flaws? Explain any problems that you can see with this theory. What is your opinion? Write down your thoughts.

Summary

You should now be able to explain what the causation argument is and how this might help somebody to believe in God.

1.5 Science and non-belief in God

Learning outcomes

By the end of this lesson you should be able to:

- outline why some people do not believe in God
- describe the scientific explanations of the origins of the universe
- explain why scientific explanations of the origins of the world may lead some people not to believe in God
- evaluate the different arguments given and express your own response to the scientific explanations of the universe, giving reasons and evidence for your opinion, and showing you understand the alternative point of view.

edexcel ⋮⋮⋮ key terms

Agnosticism – Not being sure whether God exists.

Atheism – Believing that God does not exist.

Many people used to believe that the Bible is literally true and that God really did create the world in six days as it says in Genesis. Today, some people still believe this, but others argue that the world was not made in the same way that the Bible says.

Activities

1 How does it say that God made the world in Genesis Chapters 1–3?

The Creation Story

On day one God said, "Let there be light." God called the light day, and the darkness he called night.

On day two, God made the sky.

On day three, God separated the land from the waters and created flowers, trees and grass.

Scientists today would argue that the world was made by the 'big bang'. If a person agrees with this theory, they may also argue that God did not make the world and therefore that God does not exist.

Some scientists have argued that the 'big bang' theory better explains the creation of the universe than the Genesis account does. The 'big bang' is a very complex theory. In its simplest form, this is the idea that an explosion of matter took place

about 15 billion years ago and, from this explosion, the universe came into being and it continues to expand and evolve without any involvement from an outside power. From this the Earth was created, and many scientists believe that the theory of evolution explains how life developed on Earth. The theory of evolution was proposed by Charles Darwin. He argued that all living things descended from common ancestors and that each generation

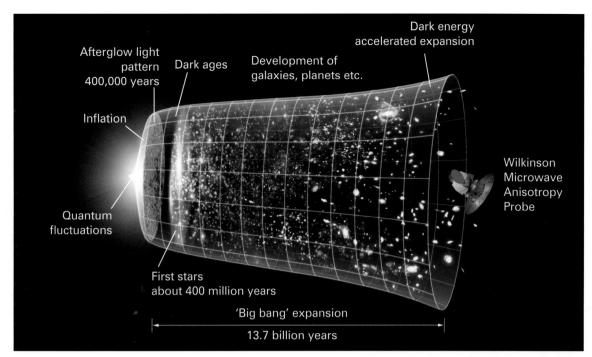

Afterglow light
pattern
400,000 years

Dark ages

Development of
galaxies, planets etc.

Dark energy
accelerated expansion

Inflation

Quantum
fluctuations

First stars
about 400 million years

Wilkinson
Microwave
Anisotropy
Probe

'Big bang' expansion

13.7 billion years

The 'big bang' timeline

has evolved from more primitive forms of life. So, for example, there may have been wolf-like creatures that evolved and developed over millions of years into the many different species of dogs we have today.

If somebody believes in these non-religious explanations, they may also argue that, if Genesis is not correct, then maybe the rest of the Bible is incorrect as well. This may lead them to doubt or to dismiss completely a faith in God.

People who do not believe in God are called atheists (this is known as **atheism**). Other people are unsure about what to believe and claim we cannot know if God exists or not. They would say that there is no way of either proving that God exists or proving that God does not exist. These people are called agnostics (this is known as **agnosticism**).

Activities

2 Imagine that you are a scientist and have been asked to give a talk to Year 10 pupils on the 'big bang' theory and non-belief in God. What would you say?

3 During the talk, one of the pupils asks why you don't believe in God. How would you answer?

Activities

Challenge

Evolution states that humans evolved from more primitive animals, and that we are continuing to evolve today. Humans are merely a more advanced animal. Some religious believers would challenge this and argue that God has made each of us and that humans are made in God's image.

4 A person who supports Darwin's theory is the atheist Richard Dawkins. Look up his work and ideas on the Internet and write a short explanation of why he does not believe in God. He uses the phrase 'purpose-coloured spectacles'. What do you think this means?

5 Research for yourself how scientists say that the 'big bang' and evolution happened. How convincing do you find these theories as opposed to the creation story? Write down your own views on this matter.

Summary

You should now be able to outline the 'big bang' and evolution and explain how scientists say the world came about. You should be able to argue why these theories may lead some people to lack faith in God.

1.6 Christian responses to scientific explanations of the world

Learning outcomes

By the end of this lesson you should be able to:

● describe the Christian responses to the scientific explanations of the universe and explain why they have these responses

● examine and evaluate the Roman Catholic viewpoint.

Do you think it is possible to believe in the Adam and Eve story and the 'big bang' theory?

There are two main responses that a Christian might give to the theory of the 'big bang'.

The literalist Christian view

There is nothing in the Bible about the 'big bang' and therefore it did not happen. The scientists are therefore wrong.

These Christians would argue that the Bible is literally the Word of God. This emphasises that every word in the Bible is totally true and that God did create the world in six days, resting on the seventh day.

If somebody were to hold this view, they would find it impossible to accept that the scientific theory of the 'big bang' is correct.

The liberal Christian view

Both the Bible and science are correct. God made the world and made the 'big bang' happen.

These Christians believe that God guided the writers of the Bible, but the people who wrote God's message down did so in their own words. Therefore, although it is true, the Bible is not meant to be taken literally. Rather, it is the message that is important not the literal meaning.

If somebody were to accept this view, they might say that the creation story was designed to teach us something about the way that God made the world and how God wants us to care for it. It is not necessarily the exact way that God made the world. These Christians may then accept the 'big bang' theory as the way that God did make the world.

Some liberal Christians say that it is possible to combine both the seven days of creation account and the 'big bang'. They say that maybe one of God's days is more like a thousand years to us. If this is the case, it would mean that the general order of the seven days of creation is followed, but over a much longer time span than one day.

'For a thousand years in your sight are like a day that has just gone by.' (Psalm 90:4)

Interestingly the 'big bang' theory's proposer, Georges Lemaître, was a Roman

Catholic priest as well as a scientist. He felt that the theory said nothing about religion. Pope Pious XII enthusiastically supported the 'big bang' theory, even before it became popular in the scientific world. The Roman Catholic Church has shown strong support for the view that the creation from nothing theory (creation *ex nihilo*) can be seen to be consistent with the 'big bang' and evolution. There is a range of views across many Churches and faith groups on this issue.

Activities

1 'The big bang made the world.'
   - Who might make this statement?
   - What do you think a person who believes the Bible is literally true might say in response to this and why?
   - What do you think a Christian who does not take the Bible literally may say in response to this and why?

For discussion

What is the most important question: How did we get here? Or why are we here?

Even if everything did evolve, surely to get a world so full of beautiful things, there must have been some greater plan?

Some Christians believe that the physical form of the world can be explained without God, but the beauty within it cannot. The world is so beautiful and mysterious that there must have been a power behind its beginning, and that must be God. How far do you agree?

ResultsPlus
Watch out!

For the exam you need to be able to give your own view, with reasons explaining your opinion. However, to get good marks you also need to recognise that others disagree with you and give reasons they would give for their point of view.

Activities

2 How do you think Georges Lemaître would respond to somebody who argued that the 'big bang' theory is not compatible with Christianity? Write his reply.

Georges Lemaître

3 Look back over the last few pages on different explanations of the origins of the world. Which is closest to your own view? Explain why.

Summary

You should now be able to say what a literalist Christian, a liberal Christian and the Roman Catholics might say in response to the 'big bang' theory and evolution.

1.7 Unanswered prayers and non-belief in God, and the Christian response

Learning outcomes

By the end of this lesson you should be able to:

● describe what is meant by unanswered prayer and how this might make someone doubt or reject the existence of God

● explore what a Christian might say to somebody who feels that God is not listening to them or does not answer their prayers

● consider some Roman Catholic viewpoints on unanswered prayer

● express your opinion on whether prayers are answered or whether they are not, and explain why this encourages you to believe or not believe in God.

edexcel ▦ key terms

Omni-benevolent – The belief that God is all-good.

Omnipotent – The belief that God is all-powerful.

Millions of people pray every day to end poverty. Why do you think that God has not answered these prayers?

An unanswered prayer is when somebody prays to God and they think that nothing has happened.

For example, somebody may pray to pass an exam, but on results day find that they have completely failed the exam. They may pray for a sick relative to be cured, but then the relative dies. Both of these are unanswered prayers.

If a person prays to God and does not get what they are asking for, they may feel that God does not exist, because if he did he would have let them have what they wanted.

Sometimes a person may pray to God and feel that God is not there. If they continue to pray and continue to feel that God is not there, then they may start to believe that God does not exist.

If this is then combined with them asking God for something that they don't get, they may lose faith completely. They may decide that God does not exist.

Many atheists are confident that if God existed, and he was **omni-benevolent** and **omnipotent**, surely he would answer everyone's prayers. Many people

Activities

1 (a) How would you feel if you continually spoke to a friend who you did not feel was listening?

(b) Do you think that this is sometimes how a person who is receiving no answer from God feels, or is it a different situation?

experience suffering and pain in their own lives or watch as family and friends suffer, and God seems to do nothing. This makes it easy for some people to reject belief in God. They see millions of people praying for the same thing all over the world, and God apparently does nothing. Some would say that this shows that God does not exist and that it is down to chance if you do get what you want.

Christian responses to unanswered prayer

Christians argue that there are many reasons why God does not seem to answer our prayers.

Some Christians will say that God does answer all our prayers but sometimes he says 'no' or 'not now'. Other Christians may argue that God does not answer prayers because some prayers are selfish, or that sometimes people do not pray for what is best for themselves or others. For example, if a person prayed to win a million pounds, this would be a selfish prayer and God would probably say 'no'.

Some Christians may argue that God answers all prayers but often not in the way that we expect. They believe that God has an ultimate plan for everyone and we cannot possibly know what that plan is. For example, if somebody were to pray to pass their exam so that they could get their dream job but they failed the exam, it would seem as though their prayer had not been answered. It could be that God did not want the person to have that dream job as they would be happier and more useful doing something else.

Portrait of St Augustine. How much do you think St Monica would have seen her son's conversion to Christianity as an answer to her prayers?

Activities

2   Imagine that you are God. Two people are praying that their team will win the football match on Saturday; however, these two people each support opposing sides. How can you answer both of them? (A draw does not count as a win!)

A Roman Catholic perspective on unanswered prayer

The Catholic Church does not take a particular line in its response to the subject of unanswered prayer. Replies may include many of the responses outlined above. Occasionally, some Catholics may ask St Monica to pray for them when their prayers go unanswered. St Monica is said to have prayed to God for a period of twenty years, asking him to help her son come to faith. At last her prayers were answered and her son eventually became St Augustine.

For more information on how Roman Catholics pray to the saints, go to www.heinemann.co.uk/ hotlinks (express code 4219P) and click on the link.

ResultsPlus
Build better answers

Explain how unanswered prayer might lead some people to reject belief in God. (8 marks)

■ **Basic, 1–2-mark answers**
Basic answers will only give one or two brief reasons or one reason with some explanation.

● **Good, 3–6-mark answers**
Good answers (3–4 marks) will give either up to four brief reasons or one developed and one brief reason or two developed reasons. Better answers (5–6 marks) will give either three developed reasons, or a couple of developed reasons along with a couple of brief reasons.

▲ **Excellent, 7–8-mark answers**
Most excellent answers give four developed reasons. Answers that give two fully-developed reasons (which means lots of explanation!) will also reach 7–8-mark answers. All excellent answers will use some key terms and good English as this is taken into account on (c) questions.

Summary

- You should now be able to explain what unanswered prayers are and why this causes some people to feel that God does not exist, or to lose faith when their prayers are not answered.

- You have also thought about a number of ways in which a Christian would respond to somebody who claims that God does not answer prayers.

1.8 Evil and suffering and non-belief in God

Learning outcomes

By the end of this lesson you should be able to:

- explain what evil is and how this might cause suffering
- describe the problem of evil and suffering for Christians
- explain why the existence of evil and suffering in the world might cause someone to doubt or reject belief in God
- give your own opinion on what suffering is, with reasons.

edexcel ⠿ key terms

Moral evil – Actions carried out by humans that cause suffering.

Natural evil – Things that cause suffering but have nothing to do with humans.

Omniscient – The belief that God knows everything that has happened and everything that is going to happen.

There are two different kinds of evil and suffering.

Moral evil

Moral evil is when somebody does something that causes harm or suffering for others, for example, in war. In a war civilians who are accidentally caught up in the war may die or lose loved ones. Their homes and other things that are valuable to them may be destroyed, causing them to suffer. The soldiers on both sides that are asked to fight in the war may experience direct suffering and the wider world experiences suffering as we see on the news what is happening there. All this has been caused by people who could have chosen to act differently but did not.

Natural evil

Natural evil is when people are suffering but the cause has nothing to do with other people. An example of this could be an earthquake. Lives and homes are destroyed, but this is due to an act of nature; it has not been caused by human beings.

Activities

1   (a) List as many types of evil and suffering as you can.

   (b) Use this list and make a note of which should be thought of as moral evil and which as natural evil.

The problem of evil and suffering

Christians argue that God is:

Omnipotent = all powerful, in which case he has the power to prevent suffering

Omniscient = all seeing/all knowing, in which case he knows what is happening

Omni-benevolent = all loving, in which case he would want to prevent suffering because he loves us.

Would a God who really loves us let us suffer?

When people are suffering they may think that God does not exist because he would otherwise have helped them. Other people may pray to God to stop the suffering and when he doesn't seem to, they may then lose faith in God or stop believing in him totally.

As there are still evil and suffering in the world, some people argue that God cannot be all of the things that Christians say that he is. They may say that God either does not have enough power to stop the suffering, or perhaps that he does have the power, but does not know that it is happening. Maybe he has the power and knows that it is happening, but just does not love us enough to make it stop. They challenge the concepts of omnipotence, **omniscience** and omni-benevolence.

If somebody chooses to accept these challenges, then it may make them lose faith in the God in whom they believed. It may make them believe that God does not exist.

Activities

2 Pretend that you are a journalist for a local religious newspaper. You need to interview somebody who has been involved in an earthquake. What would you ask?

3 Now imagine that you are that person who has been involved in the earthquake. How would you answer those questions?

4 Write the diary account of somebody who has been involved in a natural disaster, explaining how this has affected their belief in God.

For discussion

Look again at the problem of evil. Could God still be God if he had one of the three qualities (omnipotence, omniscience or omni-benevolence) missing?

Activities

Challenge

Sometimes moral and natural evils may overlap. For example, a drought that causes many people to die may at first appear as a natural evil. However, perhaps the drought had been caused by people's actions (for example, think about the possible causes of global warming). If this is the case, then the drought becomes a moral evil.

5 **(a)** For homework watch the news this evening (or look through a newspaper) and categorise the stories into those about moral evil and natural evil.

(b) From this list, identify how many of these stories could have been prevented by humans had they chosen to behave differently.

Summary

You should now be able to explain what suffering is, the difference between moral and natural evil, and also explain what the problem of evil is.

1.9 Christian responses to evil and suffering

Learning outcomes

By the end of this lesson, you should be able to:

● describe ways in which Christians, including Roman Catholics, attempt to solve the problem of evil and suffering

● explain how the Bible teaches that evil and suffering were brought into the world through human sinfulness

● give your own opinions about the problem of evil and whether it disproves the existence of God.

Some Christians may say that we should not worry about why there is evil and suffering. God has a plan for the world and it is obviously part of the plan, so we must place our faith in God and trust that he knows what is best for us, even if we do not understand it at the time.

> 'For my thoughts are not your thoughts, neither are your ways my ways,' declares the LORD. 'As the heavens are higher than the earth, so are my ways higher than your ways and my thoughts than your thoughts.' (Isaiah 55:8–9)

Instead we should follow the example of Jesus and work to combat the effects of evil and suffering with prayer and service.

Prayer

Many Christians would say that the first thing that we should do is pray, because prayer is very powerful. At times, we will be unable to do anything practical to help those who are suffering, so the only thing that we can do is pray for them.

edexcel key terms

Free will – The idea that human beings are free to make their own choices.

Service

Christians would say that when we see evil and suffering, it is a good opportunity to provide service to others, as Jesus would have done. For example, when there is an earthquake, there are many appeals for people to donate money, clothes and so on. Or if somebody is grieving, we may perceive that there is an opportunity to be a good friend to them.

Activities

1 Why do you think that 'prayer and service' may be a good motto for a Christian?

Why do you think that a Christian may choose to become a counsellor? Can you think of any other similar jobs that they may choose to do?

In addition to the idea of prayer and service, the views in the following spider diagram are held by a range of Christian believers, including those in the Roman Catholic Church.

Free will
Many Christians hold the opinion that evil and suffering are not brought about by God but by humans themselves. God has given the human race the gift of **free will** – he does not want us to be robots and serve him because we don't have any other choice. He wants us to choose to love and serve him because we want to. However, this also means that we can choose not to do what we know is the right thing, and that when we choose to do wrong this will inevitably bring pain and suffering to others.

PRAYER AND SERVICE

Not in paradise yet!
Other Christians may hold the view that there continues to be evil and suffering in the world as we are not yet in paradise. We cannot expect this world to be as pain-free and blissful as Heaven will be and therefore we should expect some pain and suffering to occur.

Life is a test
Some Christians may say that we are being tested to see if we are worthy of Heaven. If there were no pain and suffering then it would be easy to have faith in God and always do the right thing.

To help us grow
Other Christians may say that evil and suffering exist to make us stronger people, and that we learn from them. For example, war is a terrible thing, but it may nevertheless teach the people who witness it to be more forgiving and less judgemental of others. It may cause us all to strive harder for peace.

For discussion

Which point do you think is the best answer to why evil and suffering exist in the world?

ResultsPlus
Exam question report

Explain how Roman Catholics respond to the problem of evil and suffering. (8 marks) June 2007

How students answered

The candidates who scored poorly on this question answered generally about the problem of evil and suffering rather than explaining how Catholics respond to it.

Most of the candidates who scored a Level 2 for this question explained one Catholic response to the problem of evil, such as 'a test from God'.

There were some excellent answers that gave a detailed response to at least two of the different ways in which Catholics deal with the problem of evil and suffering.

Activities

2 Think about the answers a Christian might give to the problem of evil and suffering. (i) Which of the answers are the most convincing and why? (ii) Which are the least convincing and why?

Challenge

3 Conduct your own research into free will, and the problem of evil and suffering. You might want to look at what St Irenaeus and St Augustine of Hippo said about free will.

Summary

At the end of this section you should be able to explain at least four answers that Christians will give in answer to the problem of evil and suffering.

1.10 The media and belief in God

Learning outcomes

By the end of this lesson you should be able to:

- describe two programmes that could affect a person's attitude to belief in God
- explain how either of these programmes might affect a person's attitude to belief in God
- evaluate the positive and negative messages sent through the media about belief in God and express your opinion on this, with reasons and evidence.

Television and the media play a huge part in most people's lives today. We usually have the television on for at least part of the day. We may listen to the radio, search the Internet or read a newspaper. Each of these forms of media has an effect on the way we see the world and each helps us to form opinions on what is happening around us.

Religion is also a huge part of some people's lives. Sometimes the media may try to provide a balanced view of religion and the debates within religion. At other times it may appear that the media is presenting a biased view, or poking fun at a certain religion and its followers.

Activities

1 Using a television listings magazine, highlight the programmes that are connected with religion or religious issues.

Let's look at an example. The television programme *Songs of Praise* is based around hymns, usually from Christianity. It also includes interviews with people who discuss their faith and sometimes it may concentrate on one aspect of belief, such as how God helps us to have courage. This may help a person to believe in God or strengthen existing belief as they can see other people worshipping, and begin to think that all of these people cannot be wrong.

However somebody else may argue that *Songs of Praise* is more likely to detract from a person's belief in God. It is a programme that is sometimes seen as being aimed at an older audience and so therefore may lead a young person to believe that God and religion is something that older people do and is not for people of their generation. Not everybody will find that worshipping God through hymns is beneficial to them; they may find that this alienates them from God, making him seem distant. Some people may also argue that worshipping God in this way means that they become disconnected from their own church community and therefore lose the support of the community which helps them to have faith in God, especially in times of hardship.

I think everyone should be able to choose if they believe in God or not, I can make my own mind up without help from the TV!

I wouldn't believe in God! Religious believers are all bizarre. Have you seen the congregation in *The Vicar of Dibley*?

The media are often criticised for only including religious broadcasts at a certain limited time during the week – referred to as 'the God slot' and usually on a Sunday. However there are many other programmes that although not specifically dedicated to religion, do include religion in them. For example some documentaries may take account of religious views and often there are religious characters in TV programmes and soap operas. This shows to the viewer that religion can permeate every aspect of daily life and the worship of God need not be confined only to a Sunday morning, therefore helping a person feel more comfortable in expressing their belief in God and helping their faith to increase. Some people, however may argue that people who are religious are often portrayed negatively within certain programmes. For example, in the programme *Father Ted* there are three priests who are portrayed as being either not very committed to their faith or ignorant of it completely. One priest drinks too much, one is very naive and seems to know little about his faith, and the other is at times portrayed as an opportunist whose sole purpose is to benefit himself. This may affect the viewers by thinking that belief in God is silly or that religious people are hypocrites.

Do you think that it is fair to Catholics to portray priests in this way? Does this programme affect a person's attitude to belief in God?

Activities

2 Choose two programmes from those you highlighted in Activity 1. Place each of them in the centre of a piece of paper. Around them, write the positive and negative messages given by this programme about belief in God.

3 Do you think these messages could affect a person's attitude to belief in God? Explain your response.

For discussion

Should religion be banned completely from the media?

Summary

In this section you have considered how religion is portrayed in the media and the issues that are connected with this. You should be able to explain the effect that the media may have on a person's faith.

Quick quiz

1 What is meant by 'omnipotent'?

2 What is meant by 'omniscient'?

3 How might a Roman Catholic family help people believe in God?

4 Give two other ways in which people may come to believe in God.

5 Give an example of how a Christian might experience a miracle.

6 What is a conversion experience?

7 What is meant by 'causation'?

8 Why do some Christians believe that scientific views are not compatible with a religious view?

9 How does the problem of evil affect the belief that God answers prayers?

10 Suggest two ways in which Christians might help to reduce suffering.

Plenary activity

Create two characters, of any age, gender, race, background or circumstances. One is an atheist, one a theist (believer in God). Using all the sections in this unit write a short report about each character, filling in their personal details as suggested above, and explaining what they believe.

For example, you could create a character named Alan, who is in his mid-30s, brought up in a Christian home, but who now describes himself as an atheist. Why has he stopped believing in God? Did he ever believe for himself? What does he think about suffering in the world, prayer, the possible causes for the origin of the world, and so on?

Try to get into the minds of these characters so they feel real to you and to someone who might read your account. Help the reader to understand why they truly hold their beliefs. Try to include something from every spread in each character's story.

Find out more

Channel Four television shows many programmes that deal with key issues of religious belief, such as those described in this section. For more information, go to www.heinemann.co.uk/hotlinks (express code 4219P). You could record some programmes and watch others. They will give you a better idea of how important religion is to people all over the world, whether they believe in God themselves or not.

Take the opportunity to pick up leaflets in churches and other places of worship or where Christians meet together. These will often deal with questions people have about faith, or they may advertise events going on there or nearby that could give you a greater insight into why people believe and what they do together. For example, many Churches run Alpha courses, which teach the fundamentals of the Christian faith. For more information about Alpha courses, go to www.heinemann.co.uk/hotlinks (express code 4219P).

Student tips

When I studied these topics for my GCSE I made sure that I knew all the key terms very well. This was so I could be sure of getting full marks for all the questions that asked for meanings of key terms, but also so I could use some of them in other answers to show my understanding of the topics. For example, I could use 'omnipotent' when writing about why religious believers have to find solutions to the problem of evil, even if there wasn't a short question that asked what that word means.

Self-evaluation checklist

How well have you understood the topics in this section? In the first column of the table below use the following code to rate your understanding:

Green – I understand this fully

Orange – I am confident I can answer most questions on this

Red – I need to do a lot more work on this topic.

In the second and third columns you need to think about:

- Whether you have an opinion on this topic and could give reasons for that opinion if asked
- Whether you can give the opinion of someone who disagrees with you and give reasons for this alternative opinion.

Content covered	My understanding is red/orange/green	Can I give my opinion?	Can I give an alternative opinion?
The importance of a Roman Catholic Christian upbringing in coming to believe in God			
Ways in which families encourage children to believe in God			
How religious communities contribute to a religious upbringing			
The nature of religious experience			
Different types of religious experience			
What people believe about religious experiences			
What is understood by the term 'miracle'			
Different types of miracles			
Why God may perform miracles			
Problems associated with miracles			
The nature of prayer			
Why believers associate prayer with the nature of God			
The design argument for the existence of God			
The argument for the existence of God based on causation			
What it means to be a theist, atheist or agnostic			
Why some people do not believe in God because they feel that science offers a better explanation of the origin of the world			
Some scientific explanations of the origin of the world			
Ways in which Christians respond to scientific explanations for the origin of the world			
The nature of evil and suffering and why it is a problem for religious believers			
Ways in which Christians attempt to solve the problem of evil and suffering			
The portrayal in the media of believing in God			

Introduction

In the exam you will see a choice of two questions on this section. Each question will include four tasks, which test your knowledge, understanding and evaluation of the material covered. A 2-mark question will ask you to define a term; a 4-mark question will ask your opinion on a point of view; an 8-mark question will ask you to explain a particular belief or idea; a 6-mark question will ask for your opinion on a point of view and ask you to consider an alternative point of view.

You have to give your opinion, but make sure you do give two clear and thought-out reasons. These can be ones you have learned in class, even if they are not your own opinion. You mustn't use terms such as 'rubbish' or 'stupid' as these don't show that you are able to think things through carefully.

Mini exam paper

1. (a) What is **atheism**?
     (2 marks)

   (b) Do you think prayer is a waste of time?
     Give **two** reasons for your point of view. (4 marks)

   (c) Explain how a religious upbringing in a Roman Catholic family can lead to belief in God. (8 marks)

   (d) *'Evil and suffering prove that God does not exist.'*
     In your answer you should refer to Roman Catholic Christianity.
     (i) Do you agree? Give reasons for your opinion. (3 marks)
     (ii) Give reasons why some people may disagree with you. (3 marks)

Here you need to give a short, accurate definition. You do not need to write more than one clear sentence.

For this question you need first to think of what a Roman Catholic upbringing involves. When you have four different things you should then explain these aspects of the upbringing, linking them to how this would then help the person to believe in God. This question is worth 8 marks so you must be prepared to spend some time answering it. You will also be assessed on your use of language in this question.

Again, you can use reasons you have learned from your studies. At this stage you only need to give one point of view, for or against.

Now you have to give the opposite point of view, again, using material you have learned during your studies. You don't have to say what you think about these alternative points of view, but you do need to show you understand why they are just as important to consider as your own opinion.

Mark scheme

(a) You can earn **2 marks** for a correct answer, and **1 mark** for a partially correct answer.

(b) To earn up to the full **4 marks** you need to give two reasons (as asked) and to develop them fully. Two brief reasons or only one developed reason will earn **2 marks**.

(c) You can earn **7–8 marks** by giving up to four reasons, but the fewer reasons you give, the more you must develop them. Because you are being assessed on use of language you also need to take care to express your understanding in a clear style of English, and make some use of specialist vocabulary.

(d) To go beyond **3 marks** for the whole of this question you must refer to Catholic Christianity. The more you are able to develop your reasons the more marks you will earn. Three simple reasons can earn you the same mark as one fully developed reason.

Results**Plus**
Maximise your marks

(b)   Do you think prayer is a waste of time? Give **two** reasons for your point of view. (4 marks)

Student answer	Examiner comments	Improved student answer
I think that prayer is not a waste of time as it is a way to make contact with God. Even though God cannot be seen or heard in the usual way, believers in God can speak to him through prayer and believe that he is listening.	The phrase 'a way to make contact with God' is good, and the answer comments on the difficulty of knowing God, with prayer offering one way of solving that difficulty.	I think that prayer is not a waste of time as it is a way to make contact with God. Even though God cannot be seen or heard in the usual way, believers in God can speak to him through prayer and believe that he is listening.
There is always the chance that he may answer the believer's prayer and make their lives better.	The candidate comes close to giving another reason by saying that prayer may make the believer's life better, but it hasn't really been explained. This answer will gain 2 marks as the candidate has given only one reason that they have developed.	Millions of people believe that God does answer their prayers and improve their lives, which strengthens their belief in God. For them, prayer is certainly not a waste of time.

Matters of life and death

Introduction

In this section you will learn about issues concerning life and death, not solely from a religious perspective, but also from that of non-believers. You will look at what Christians – and at what Roman Catholics in particular – believe happens to them after death. You will also consider how we deal with life on Earth. You will explore how people value life and what steps they take to protect and enhance it.

Learning outcomes for this section

By the end of this section you should be able to:

- give definitions of the key terms and understand how to use them to answer GCSE questions
- explain why Roman Catholics believe in life after death and how this belief affects their lives
- understand non-religious belief in life after death (near-death experiences, ghosts, mediums, evidence of reincarnation)
- explain why some people do not believe in life after death
- understand the Roman Catholic view on the sanctity of life
- outline the current law on abortion and explain why it generates such debate
- explain the different Christian attitudes to abortion and the reasons for them
- understand what is meant by euthanasia, the law on euthanasia and the different situations in which it is raised
- describe the Christian attitudes to euthanasia and explain why people have these opinions
- describe the causes of world poverty
- understand how and why CAFOD is trying to end world poverty
- explain how the media deals with life and death issues and how an issue is presented in the media
- evaluate whether the media's treatment of these issues is fair to religious beliefs and religious people.

---

edexcel ::: key terms

abortion	**immortality of the soul**	**paranormal**	**resurrection**
assisted suicide	**near-death experience**	**quality of life**	**sanctity of life**
euthanasia	**non-voluntary euthanasia**	**reincarnation**	**voluntary euthanasia**

Fascinating fact

80 per cent of British people think that people suffering terminal illness should be able to ask for help to die if they want to. (From a Dying with Dignity survey.)

1   What do you believe happens to people after death? Discuss your opinions with the person next to you.

2   Why do you think people believe in life after death?

3   Do you think that doctors should be allowed to help people to die? Explain your answer.

2.1 Roman Catholic beliefs in life after death and how these affect their lives

Learning outcomes

By the end of this lesson you should be able to:

● describe why Roman Catholics believe in life after death

● explain what Roman Catholics believe happens to them after death

● explain how these beliefs affect the way they live their lives

● give your own opinion on life after death.

edexcel ⋮⋮⋮ key terms

Immortality of the soul – The idea that the soul lives on after the death of the body.

Resurrection – The belief that, after death, the body stays in the grave until the end of the world when it is raised.

Most religions include teachings about what they believe happens after death. People have different ideas about what form this will take, but what many do accept is that the things we have done in this life will have a consequence on what happens to us after death and in the afterlife.

Jesus said:

'I am the resurrection and the life. He who believes in me will live, even though he dies; and whoever lives and believes in me will never die.' (John 11:25–26)

The resurrection of Jesus gives Catholics hope of eternal life.

Activities

1 What do you think it is about death that people fear?

2 Why do you think people believe in life after death?

For Christians, the belief in an afterlife comes from the death and **resurrection** of Jesus. St Paul taught that those people who believe in Jesus and the resurrection must believe that they can also look forward to an afterlife. To Christians, the resurrection is not just something that happened to someone a long time ago. It is a sign of the power of Jesus, even over death. Christians believe that Jesus made it possible for them to have life after death in Heaven through his death and resurrection.

Activities

3 Explain why Christians think Jesus rising from the dead proves there is life after death.

4 Do you think that life after death is possible? What form do you think it will take? Write down some words that describe your thoughts.

The parable of the sheep and the goats (Matthew 25:31–46) is a reminder that the way people live in this life determines where they will spend eternity. The teaching of the Roman Catholic Church speaks of three different destinations after death and judgement. One is temporary and two are permanent.

> **Heaven** – a place of paradise where God rules.
>
> **Hell** – a place of horrors where Satan rules.
>
> **Purgatory** – a place of waiting and preparation. This is for people who do not go straight to Heaven as they have unpurified souls. People on Earth can pray for those in Purgatory.

Catholic Christians believe:

- that the soul of a Christian who has not sinned since their last confession will go straight to Heaven
- in the **immortality of the soul** – that the soul lives on after the death of the body
- that there is 'life everlasting', as stated in the Creed and Catechism.

The Creed and the Catechism teach that Jesus will come back to Earth and raise the dead and all the souls will be reunited with their bodies. Then God will judge the living and the dead, and a new Heaven and a new Earth will be made where the resurrected souls from Heaven and Purgatory will live forever.

The soul of a Christian who has unforgiven sins and, possibly, good members of other faiths or good people who did not know of God will go to Purgatory to be cleansed of their sins. Roman Catholics believe this because the Catechism teaches:

'All who die in God's grace and friendship, but still imperfectly purified are indeed assured of their eternal salvation; but after death they undergo purification, so as to achieve the holiness necessary to enter Heaven.' (Catechism of the Catholic Church, 1033)

Those who do not believe in God and have rejected him or have committed unforgivable sins will go to Hell.

Roman Catholics believe these teachings and they affect the way in which they live their lives because:

- Christians believe that they will be judged by God after death, so they live their lives within the guidelines of the Bible. These have an impact on their personal relationships and how they treat others.
- The fact that Jesus rose from the dead gives them hope that they too will rise and be rewarded with eternal life.
- It offers comfort for those who might be grieving; they know that a place of paradise awaits their loved ones.
- Jesus's resurrection from the dead gives people hope that they can be forgiven of the sins they have committed and that they can work towards a better future.

Activities

Challenge

5   Explain why Catholics believe in life after death.

6   Imagine you are helping a friend to come to terms with bereavement. What teachings of the Catholic Church would you stress to help them?

For discussion

Catholics believe that God is good and kind – do you think that the idea of Hell goes against this view? Explain your opinion.

Summary

Catholics believe in an afterlife. This is because the resurrection of Jesus confirms that good overcomes evil and the power of God overcomes death. They believe all those who are perfectly pure will go to Heaven, those with unforgiven sins will go to Purgatory and those who have rejected God will go to Hell.

2.2 Non-religious belief in life after death

Learning outcomes

By the end of this lesson you should be able to:

- outline the reasons non-religious people believe in life after death
- understand why they believe there is an afterlife
- describe a near-death experience
- evaluate the evidence and express your own opinion with supporting reasons.

edexcel ::: key terms

Near-death experience – When someone who is about to die has an out-of-body experience.

Paranormal – Unexplained things that are thought to have spiritual causes, e.g. ghosts or mediums.

Reincarnation – The belief that, after death, souls are reborn in a new body.

Activities

1 Make a list of the reasons why a person might believe in life after death.
2 Pick three statements from those shown and develop them further.
3 Using the remaining three statements, develop arguments against them.

Many people claim not to believe in God nor do they belong to any religious group, yet they have a strong belief that there will be another life after they die.

'My Nan spoke to my dead granddad through a medium, so that proves there is life after death.'

'Ghosts prove that people can live after death, just in a different form.'

'There has to be something after death or it makes life seem pointless.'

'Belief in an afterlife gives me comfort and hope.'

'Near-death experiences show that life after death exists.'

'There has to be a place for those who have led good lives to be rewarded and for those who have been bad to be punished.'

Do you think ghosts are proof that there is life after death?

People without a faith have different views about what happens when we die; they base their answers around several possibilities.

Presence of a spirit world, e.g. ghosts and supernatural events

People such as mediums claim to be able to make contact with the dead. This is a custom that was around in Old Testament times. We know this because the Old Testament book Leviticus details how the practice was banned.

'A man or woman who is a medium or spiritist among you must be put to death.' (Leviticus 20:27)

Some people claim to have **paranormal** abilities, such as being able to contact those who are dead; they call themselves mediums or psychics. They hold seances where people ask them to contact members of their family. Some television channels now even broadcast programmes such as *Ghost Hunting* where mediums look for and pass on messages from the dead.

Near-death experiences

People who claim to have had a **near-death experience** report seeing a tunnel or bright light. Others recall looking down from the ceiling at medical staff. These events normally happen to patients who have been pronounced dead for a very small amount of time. This then convinces them that there is an afterlife.

There is at present no proof to support people's claims of near-death experiences, and the Roman Catholic Church does not accept these as proof of an afterlife. However, doctors at 25 UK and US hospitals will study 1,500 survivors to see if people with no heartbeat or brain activity can have 'out of body' experiences.

To test this the researchers have set up special shelving in resuscitation areas. The shelves hold pictures – but they are visible only from the ceiling.

Dr Sam Parnia, who is heading the study, said:

'If you can demonstrate that consciousness continues after the brain switches off, it allows for the possibility that the consciousness is a separate entity. It is unlikely that we will find many cases where this happens, but we have to be open-minded. And if no one sees the pictures, it shows these experiences are illusions or false memories.'

Evidence of reincarnation

Reincarnation is the belief that a person's soul is reborn into another body when they die. This is often seen as a religious experience – as it is believed by Hindus and Sikhs – but many non-religious people also believe in reincarnation, often because of *déjà vu*, or memories from past lives.

ResultsPlus
Top tip!

The (b) questions in the exam will ask 'What do you think about…?' The marks are awarded for the reasons you give for holding this opinion. Be aware of the difference between stating/describing what you think and the reasons why you think it!

For discussion

How would you prove a near-death experience?

Activities

4   Do you think that mediums can really contact the dead? Give reasons for your opinion.
5   Which of the views on life after death do you find the most convincing and why?

Summary

Many people believe that a person's spirit continues to live on after the human body has died. They do not necessarily base this belief on a religion but on events that occur in their lives such as near-death experiences, déjà vu or their exposure to mediums and the spirit world.

2.3 Non-belief in life after death

Learning outcomes

By the end of this lesson you should be able to:

● outline and explain why some people do not believe in life after death

● evaluate the evidence presented and communicate your own opinion and reasons for it.

Some people see death as a full stop, the end, there is nothing to follow from it.

Many non-religious people do not believe in life after death. They believe that once the body dies, that is the end. This can be for several reasons:

● They believe that there is no proof of life after death.

● They wonder 'Where could this life after death physically be? We are able to travel beyond our planet and we still have not found it.'

● They believe that religion offers no good reason to believe in life after death.

● They believe that science provides better answers, making life after death impossible.

● They believe that mediums and other people who attempt to prove life after death are just tricking people and giving them false hope.

● They believe that when a person dies the body rots, so how can they live again?

● They believe life after death is simply impossible – we are either alive or dead.

Activities

2 Is it possible to believe in life after death without believing in God? Explain your answer.

Activities

1 Many Christians see death as more of a comma, a pause before the journey to eternal life. Explain why some people see death as a full stop – the end.

For some people, it is the concepts of Heaven and Hell that make them not believe in religion and life after death. They find the concepts outdated and feel that they are a way in which religion can control the behaviour of its followers.

Activities

3 Use the table below to give reasons to support each view. You can then use this information when you are answering a GCSE question.

A Christian would give the following reasons for believing in life after death	A person who does not believe in God would give the following reasons for not believing in life after death

Do images of Hell encourage or dispel belief in an afterlife?

Centuries ago some Christian Churches used the idea of Hell to frighten people into leading a good life and following the instructions of the Church. They were warned that if they did not they risked eternal damnation in Hell.

ResultsPlus
Exam question report

Explain why some people do not believe in life after death. (8 marks) June 2007

How students answered

Many students scored poorly on this question because they answered very vaguely. Some wrote about why people do believe in life after death, which would have received no marks.

These answers generally offered one developed reason or a couple of brief reasons, but not enough to gain high marks.

There were a few students who gave excellent answers to this question. They either gave three or four reasons, or developed at least two reasons.

Summary

Some people find it impossible to believe in an afterlife – they find no proof of its existence and they believe that to be alive is to be physical and mortal, not spiritual and immortal.

2.4 Teaching on the sanctity of life

Learning outcomes

By the end of this lesson you should be able to:

- understand the concept of the sanctity of life
- outline Roman Catholic teaching on the sanctity of life.

edexcel ⋙ key terms

Sanctity of life – The belief that life is holy and belongs to God.

Christians believe that life is God-given and is a gift that is holy and belongs to God; they call this the **sanctity of life**. Christians believe that humans are made in the image of God and are responsible for His creation.

Roman Catholics believe that life is sacred because of the life, death and resurrection of Jesus. They believe that:

- human life is holy and must be protected
- they must make it their duty to protect and preserve human life, as they believe that only God has the power to give and to take life.

Other reasons why Catholics believe in the sanctity of life include:

- the commandment that states 'Do not kill'. This teaches that it is wrong to take away life
- the Bible teaching that God created all humans in his image and saw that life was good
- the Catechism that teaches Catholics that nobody has the right to take away another person's life.

'Before I formed you in the womb I knew you.' (Jeremiah 1:5)

'If we live, it is for the Lord that we live, and if we die, it is for the Lord that we die. So whether we live or die we belong to the Lord.' (Romans 14:8)

'Before I formed you in the womb I knew you, before you were born I set you apart.' (Jeremiah 1:5)

Activities

1 Explain using your own words what is meant by the term the 'sanctity of life'.

2 Using the information above, explain why you think Catholics are opposed to abortion and euthanasia.

36

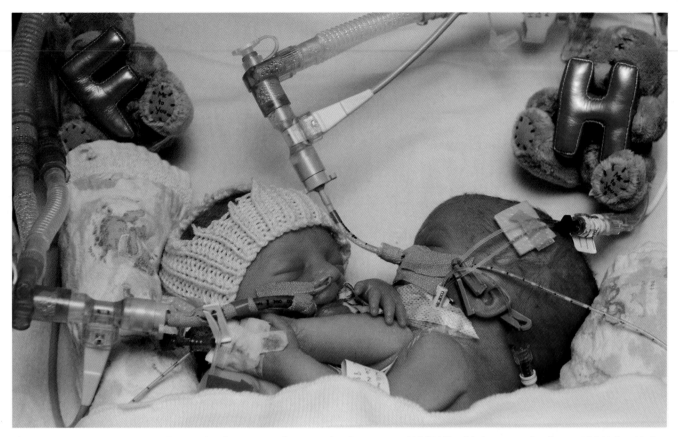

Conjoined twins are rare and figures for them range from one in about every 200,000 live births to one in about 400,000 live births.

In November 2008, eighteen-year-old Laura Williams gave birth to conjoined twins Faith and Hope, who were joined at the chest and shared a liver but had separate hearts. Laura and her husband found out about their children's condition at a routine 12-week scan. They were offered a termination based upon the medical problems that the twins might suffer, which they declined. Doctors were forced to perform an operation to separate the twins at just a week old, the result being that both babies eventually died.

ResultsPlus
Top tip!

The concept and teachings on sanctity of life are very important to Catholics and other Christians and influence their opinions on abortion and euthanasia. The best answers to questions about religious opinions and attitudes towards abortion and euthanasia will mention the concept of sanctity of life. Remember to apply it in your own answers!

For discussion

- Discuss what you think people should do when they know that their unborn child might be born with medical problems.
- Why do you think Laura Williams chose to continue with her pregnancy?
- What advice do you think a Roman Catholic would give a person who was unsure about their pregnancy?

Summary

The sanctity of life teaches that all life is sacred and belongs to God. This teaching influences Catholics' views on abortion and euthanasia as they believe life is precious and should be preserved.

2.5 The nature of abortion and abortion legislation

Learning outcomes

By the end of this lesson you should be able to:

- understand what is meant by abortion
- describe the law on abortion
- explain the different views on abortion
- outline the arguments for and against abortion.

edexcel ⠿ key terms

Abortion – The removal of a foetus from the womb before it can survive.

When does life begin?

An **abortion** is the term given to a procedure that ends the life of a foetus (unborn child) while it is still in the womb.

Abortion has always been a highly controversial issue. Almost everybody has an opinion on it. Some form this from a religious viewpoint while others believe that it is a woman's right to decide. Many people's opinions on abortion are affected by when they believe human life begins – there is a huge range of opinions, from those who say a foetus is a human life from the moment that it is conceived to those who say that it is not a human life until it is born.

The UK law on abortion

Abortion became legal in the UK in 1967. The 1967 Abortion Act and Human Fertilisation and Embryology Act of 1990 together form the current abortion law in the UK. All abortions must be agreed by two doctors and be carried out in an NHS or private hospital or an approved and legal clinic.

Under the existing law an abortion can take place up to the *24th week of pregnancy*, if two doctors agree that:	Abortion is allowed *after 24 weeks* if there is:
• continuing with the pregnancy would pose a risk to the physical or mental health of the mother • if the child were to be born then it would be seriously or mentally disabled • the existing children of the mother may suffer physically or mentally if a new baby is born	• a risk to the life of the mother • evidence that the baby will be severely disabled if it is born • evidence that the woman will be at serious risk of physical or mental injury

Abortion Rights

Some people think that abortion is acceptable – they believe that it is the woman's right to choose; these people are called 'pro-choice'.

- They believe that it is the woman's right to decide what happens to her own body.

- They argue that in cases such as rape, where the child might be unwanted, a termination is the better option to prevent the mother and child from experiencing any long-term mental illness.

- They also argue that a termination may be the better option when the mother may not be able to give the child an adequate standard of living, for example if she is too young and not ready to be a mother.

They claim that if abortions were made illegal then many women would be forced to seek backstreet abortions and risk their own health.

Pro Life

Some people believe that abortion is not acceptable and they believe that the unborn child has a right to life – they are called 'pro-life'.

- They believe that life begins at conception and that all life is special and should not be taken away.

- They argue that the unborn child should have the same rights as any human being.

- They promote adoption and the fact that loving parents can be found for the child.

- They argue that disabled children are of the same importance as able-bodied children and can live happy and fulfilling lives.

Changes to the law

Abortion law is frequently under debate in Parliament. MPs recently voted against lowering the time permitted for a termination from 24 weeks to 20 weeks. Many people who are against abortion ('pro-life') argue that the limit should be 18 weeks, as premature babies can survive at less than 24 weeks. Pro-choice supporters argue that abortion should be allowed up to 24 weeks as it is the woman's right to choose to have an abortion.

Activities

1. Using your own words, outline, in a paragraph, the current law on abortion in the UK.

2. Can you think of any circumstances under which someone might not be granted an abortion before 24 weeks? For example, they may wish to terminate their pregnancy as they have found out they are having a boy and they wanted a girl. Share these answers with the person next to you.

3. Do you think that doctors should have to carry out abortions if they do not want to?

4. Is a mother's life more important than the foetus? Give reasons to support your answer.

Summary

Abortion is the termination and removal of a foetus from the womb. It is legal in the UK to have an abortion up to 24 weeks and in certain circumstances beyond this date. Abortion is a very emotive issue with many being 'pro-life' and others being 'pro-choice'.

2.6 Christian views on abortion

Learning outcomes

By the end of this lesson you should be able to

- outline Christian beliefs on abortion
- explain why Christians have different attitudes towards abortion
- decide your own point of view on abortion.

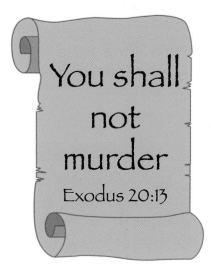

Are there any cases where you think this command might not apply?

Activities

1 We have already seen that Christians believe in the sanctity of life. Using what you have learned about this, explain what you think a Christian would think about abortion.

Abortion is an emotive topic, and like all people, different Christians have different views. The table on the next page shows some points of view on abortion and who believes them. It then explains why they have that view – the 'why' section will help you in understanding questions.

Results Plus
Build better answers

'Abortion is never right, whatever the circumstances.'

In your answer, you should refer to Roman Catholic Christianity.

(i) Do you agree? Give reasons for your opinion. (3 marks)

■ Basic, 1-mark answers
These answers will offer an opinion with a basic reason. Be aware of the difference between saying what you think, and giving reasons why you think it.

● Good, 2-mark answers
These will either offer two basic reasons for an opinion or one well-developed reason.

▲ Excellent, 3-mark answers
The best answers will either give three simple reasons or two reasons with some explanation or a fully developed reason.

(ii) Give reasons why some people may disagree with you. (3 marks)

■ Basic, 1-mark answers
These answers will offer an opinion with a basic reason.

● Good, 2-mark answers
These will either offer two basic reasons for their opinion or one well-developed reason.

▲ Excellent, 3-mark answers
The best answers will either give three simple reasons or two reasons with some explanation or a fully developed reason.

View	Who	Why
Against abortion	The Catholic Church Evangelical Christians	• They believe that life begins at conception (the moment the sperm meets the egg) and the foetus is made in the image of God and is alive. • The Ten Commandments teach not to take life, so abortion is wrong. • The Catechism of the Catholic Church teaches that 'Abortion is a horrible crime… a deliberate violation of the child's rights'. • God has a plan for every person and no human should interfere with God's plan. • Adoption is a better option as the child can be given to loving parents. • If women have abortions because their child would be born disabled, this is in conflict with those who are disabled and lead fulfilling lives. • The Catholic Church does accept that there are special cases that doctors might be faced with, for example the pregnant mother has cancer and the treatment for the cancer would kill the foetus. In this case, Catholics look to the doctrine of 'double effect'. The first effect is to save the life of the mother and the double effect of this is the death of the foetus. However, the aim was not the death of the unborn child but the saving of the mother's life.
Believes that abortion is wrong but will allow it in some circumstances	The Church of England	• They allow abortion if they believe that it is the most loving thing to do, for example if the mother has been a victim of rape or if the pregnancy would put the mother's life at risk. Jesus told people to love their neighbour as themselves, so they accept that at times and under certain circumstances abortion is the most loving thing to do. • They do not believe that life begins at conception. • The sanctity of life is broken in events such as war, so they believe that it can be broken in a just abortion where the mother's life is at risk.
Against abortion but allows it as the lesser of two evils	Liberal protestants such as some Methodists	• They believe that Jesus treated people with love and compassion so they must do the same. • God gave humans free will and people must make decisions for themselves. • Medical advances allow early detection of conditions and disabilities so abortions should be permitted to prevent suffering. • Christianity is based on justice and if abortion was against the law many women would seek backstreet abortions. This would mean that those unable to pay would suffer.

Activities

2 What arguments can you think of for abortion? Discuss this as a class and share ideas.

3 Create a table with one column headed 'For abortion' and a second column headed 'Against abortion'. In the first column write down the arguments for abortion you have identified with the class in the activity above. Add in anything else you can think of. In the second column write down all the arguments against abortion you can think of.

4 Explain why there are different attitudes to abortion in Christianity.

5 State your own view on abortion and why you hold that opinion.

Summary

• Catholics and evangelical Christians believe that abortion is always wrong as life belongs to God and they view abortion as murder.

• The Church of England and liberal Christians allow abortion as the lesser of two evils, seeing it overall as the most loving thing to do.

2.7 The nature of euthanasia

Learning outcomes

By the end of this lesson you should be able to:

- understand what is meant by euthanasia
- be able to describe different forms of euthanasia
- explain why some people are against euthanasia
- explain why some support the legalisation of euthanasia.

edexcel ::: key terms

Assisted suicide – Providing a seriously ill person with the means to commit suicide.

Euthanasia – The painless killing of someone dying from a painful disease.

Non-voluntary euthanasia – Ending someone's life painlessly when they are unable to ask, but you have good reason for thinking they would want you to do so.

Quality of life – The idea that life must have some benefits for it to be worth living.

Voluntary euthanasia – Ending life painlessly when someone in great pain asks for death.

What is euthanasia?

Euthanasia is sometimes called 'mercy killing'. It means to bring about death more quickly by the use of drugs, neglect, suffocation or some other method, with or without the person's consent in order to relieve their suffering.

It means that a human person makes a decision that life should end. Christianity teaches us that life is a gift from God and that it is God who decides the moment of death. It emphasises that natural death should be allowed to occur.

There are several types of euthanasia and several ways in which it may be carried out:

- **Voluntary euthanasia** is carried out at the request of the patient. It is this type of euthanasia that is legal in some countries.
- **Non-voluntary euthanasia** is ending someone's life painlessly when they are unable to ask, though you have good reason for thinking they would want you to do so.
- In a case of **assisted suicide**, someone helps the patient to end their life.
- Active euthanasia is carried out by a doctor performing a deliberate action, such as a legal injection.
- Passive euthanasia is carried out when medical treatment or life support is deliberately withdrawn or when a severely ill or handicapped baby is not given treatment that would help them to survive.

Switching off a life-support machine for a patient who has already been tested and is declared 'brain dead' is not considered euthanasia and is permissible in the UK.

Activities

1 Is it right to ask a doctor to help you die? Give reasons for your opinion.

In the UK all forms of euthanasia are against the law and anyone involved in them can be sent to prison. However, some countries, such as the Netherlands and Switzerland, have made euthanasia legal if the patients, their relatives and two doctors agree to it.

Arguments that support euthanasia

Many people are in favour of euthanasia and want the law to be changed, they believe:

- a person should be allowed to make decisions about their own life
- it allows a person to die with dignity rather than suffer

Matt Hampson (left) and Dan James (right) were both paralysed in rugby training accidents. Dan travelled to a clinic in Switzerland where he committed assisted suicide. His parents were with him. Matt's response to this was 'You get busy living or get busy dying. Me? I chose to live.' (The Sunday Times, 19 October 2008).

- medicines keep people alive who previously would have died, but with a poor **quality of life**
- it saves on medical costs
- it stops families having to watch people die slowly and painfully.

Activities

2 What message do you think the death of Dan James sends out to those people who are disabled?

3 Do you think that Dan's parents should be prosecuted for helping their son to die?

4 What do you understand by the statement, 'Get busy living or get busy dying'?

5 Read the different arguments for and against euthanasia on this page. Which do you think is the most 'important' argument for euthanasia? Which is the most 'important' argument against it? Explain your decisions.

Non-religious arguments against euthanasia

Many people argue that euthanasia should remain illegal because:

- a doctor's job is to save lives not end them
- the patient–doctor relationship would change – if euthanasia was legal, patients might not believe their doctors were doing everything possible to save them
- ill or elderly people might be forced into committing euthanasia by selfish relatives
- it is not possible to assess if people are of sound mind when they ask for euthanasia
- hospices can provide full and adequate care for the dying
- a cure might be found for their illness.

ResultsPlus
Build better answers

What is assisted suicide? (2 marks)

Good, 1-mark answers
These answers will offer partially correct definitions such as 'helping someone die'.

Excellent, 2-mark answers
The best answers will provide a simple, but full definition such as the one given in the key terms panel.

Summary

Euthanasia is against the law in the UK. There are many different types of euthanasia; many people are campaigning for voluntary euthanasia to be allowed in the UK.

43

2.8 Evaluate the different Christian views on euthanasia

44

Learning outcomes

By the end of this lesson you should be able to:

● understand different Christian attitudes to euthanasia

● explain why Christians hold these different views

● give your own opinion and reasons for it.

Catholic Christianity teaches that life is a gift from God and that it is God who decides the moment of death. Natural death should be allowed to occur. This view is based on the belief in the sanctity of life, which comes from the teaching that all people were made in the image of God and that it is for him only to give and take life.

Pope John Paul II described euthanasia as 'a grave violation of the law of God'. Christians are concerned to protect people who feel they may be a burden on others and who may be under pressure to seek a speeding up of their own death. They are aware, too, of the weight of responsibility on doctors and how euthanasia may change the patient–doctor relationship. Many Christians do not believe it is always right to use modern technology to prolong life at all costs, and they draw a distinction between allowing death to occur when treatment is pointless and when death is caused deliberately.

Activities

1 Explain why the sanctity of life is important to Christians.

2 If euthanasia became legal what problems might occur?

3 How do you think a Christian would respond to Debbie Purdy's request?

4 'Everyone has the right to control what happens to their own body.' Do you agree? Explain your view and think of an alternative opinion to yours.

Debbie Purdy, who has multiple sclerosis, launched a bid to ensure that her husband is not prosecuted for helping her to travel abroad to end her life.

ResultsPlus
Watch out!

Remember that although individual Christians may have different attitudes to euthanasia, no Christian Church in the UK will support it. Many students get confused and say that different 'Churches' have different opinions, which is not the case!

Although all Christians believe that life is precious, they have differing views on euthanasia.

Roman Catholic, evangelical and most conservative Christians believe that euthanasia is WRONG because:

- It is taking away a life and is against the commandment 'Do not murder'.

- God created humans in his image and only He has the power to take away life.

- No person should value themselves as so worthless that it would be better to die.

- It is against the Catechism of the Roman Catholic Church.

- They believe that it is up to medical experts to determine when death has occurred. If the medical experts state that a person is brain dead, however, then Catholics believe that life has already ended, and so switching off a machine is accepting that death has occurred and is not euthanasia.

- The Roman Catholic Church will allow various pain reliefs to ease suffering. These might shorten a person's life but that is not the aim. It is the intention to relieve pain, not to shorten life. This is the doctrine of double effect.

Other Christian views on euthanasia

Some Christians take the teachings of the Bible literally so this influences their views.

- The Bible bans suicide and they believe that all forms of euthanasia are suicide and therefore wrong.

- They believe that if a human ends a life they are putting themselves on a par with God, which is condemned in the Bible.

- They do not permit the switching off of a life support machine, the refusal of treatment or the prescribing of large pain killers to speed up death as they believe it goes against the commandment, 'Do not murder'.

A minority of liberal Christians are in favour of euthanasia. They say that there is nothing in the Bible that states that a person must be kept alive at all costs. Jesus summarised the commandments of the Bible with the two Great Commandments (Matthew 22:34–40) as *'love God'* and *'love your neighbour as yourself'*. These Christians say that sometimes it is the most loving thing to do to allow a terminally ill patient to have an easy and gentle death, which is euthanasia.

Activities

5 Explain the different Christian attitudes to euthanasia.

6 Why might euthanasia be seen by some people to be the most loving thing to do?

Summary

Most Christians are opposed to euthanasia as they believe that life is a gift from God that must be preserved and valued. Christians work to ensure that those who are dying are offered adequate care that prepares them for death and promotes human dignity.

2.9 The causes of world poverty

Learning outcomes

By the end of this section you should be able to:

● explain the terms LEDC and MEDC

● outline the causes of world poverty

● understand the differences that exist between countries.

Reference to countries	Why they are called this
LEDC (Less Economically Developed Countries) – This is a title given to those countries that are less wealthy and are underdeveloped. Examples of countries that are classed as LEDCs are Ethiopia, Bangladesh and Zimbabwe.	• They frequently suffer from famine. • They suffer from natural disasters that destroy their fragile economies. • They have a low life expectancy. • They have poor quality of life and need the support of richer nations to help them.
MEDC (More Economically Developed Countries) – These are wealthy, more powerful countries. Countries that are classed as MEDCs include the UK, USA, Australia and France.	• They have enough and often surplus food in their country. • They do not experience as many natural disasters. • They have a high life expectancy. • They have high quality of life and are often owed money in debt repayments from poorer nations.

A child victim of famine in southern Sudan, 1993.

Activities

1 Look at the picture on the left. What questions about life and death do you think it raises?

2 Why do you think the child might be in this situation? Make a list of the reasons you can think of.

3 The photographer was awarded a prize for taking this image. Do you think that was right? Explain your answer.

World poverty is not caused by one single factor; it is usually a combination of events that contribute to making a country poor. The diagram opposite shows some of the main causes of poverty.

Corrupt governments
Some LEDCs suffer at the hands of their government leaders, who receive aid and assistance from other countries; through corruption this money does not reach the people who need it the most. Also some governments allow the population to suffer as they then have less energy and resources to threaten the government's control.

Dirty water
Many people living in LEDCs do not have access to clean drinking water; they are faced with the choice of drinking unclean water and risking disease or dying of dehydration. Many children die of stomach upsets caused by dirty water. The lack of health care, education and basic facilities also prevent a country from developing.

HIV and Aids
In many LEDCs the spread of HIV and Aids has destroyed communities. In Zambia, it is estimated that almost half the population will die of HIV or Aids. The medicines used to control the disease in the West are too expensive for the people to buy. The illness prevents people from working and leaves children without parents and therefore without an income. The children often have to work to support those younger in the family, and as a result they miss out on an education and the opportunity to work themselves out of the poverty trap.

War
Many LEDCs suffer from war. The effects of war destroy homes, schools, crops and buildings. As a result communities and families are broken up. People are unable to work or be educated. War also creates refugees; these people may seek refuge in a neighbouring country. The sudden influx of refugees who have no money or food with them can make the country they arrive in poor.

Causes of world poverty

Debt
LEDCs suffer from debt as they have borrowed money from banks in MEDCs; they then struggle to make the repayments on the loans when interest rises. Any money the country does have has to go towards loan repayments, meaning that the country cannot develop or work its way out of poverty.

Natural disasters
Many LEDCs are in regions where they regularly suffer from disasters such as earthquakes, floods and drought. As a result homes and crops are destroyed. The fragile economy of the country is unable to support those suffering, so they are trapped further in a cycle of poverty. As a consequence, they grow cash crops to sell and then pay towards their debt rather than feeding the people.

Activities

Challenge
5   Some people argue that abortion and euthanasia are justified for those who do not have a good quality of life. How does this rule apply to those people who are suffering from a poor quality of life due to poverty, in the developing world and in the UK? Is it fair to use the same arguments?

Summary

World poverty is not caused by one single factor; it is a combination of events and circumstances that affect a country and destroy its development. Some countries, such as Mexico, are making good progress and have moved on in their development, whereas others, such as Zimbabwe, have fallen further into decline.

Activities

4   How many of the problems faced by LEDCs are manmade? Discuss how you think these problems could be solved.

2.10 Understand how and why CAFOD is trying to end world poverty

Learning outcomes

By the end of this lesson you should be able to:

- explain why CAFOD works to help end world poverty
- outline how it helps
- describe different examples of CAFOD's work.

What is CAFOD and why does it help?

CAFOD is the major Catholic Charity in England and Wales that works to end world poverty. CAFOD stands for Catholic Agency for Overseas Development.

CAFOD believes that all human beings have a right to dignity and respect, and that the world's resources are a gift to be shared equally by all men and women, whatever their race, nationality or religion. CAFOD wants people to help others with compassion, solidarity, stewardship and hope.

CAFOD is inspired by the teachings in the Bible and the Church's social teaching. Through helping those who are suffering they are putting their faith into action.

Catholics believe that God created the universe and appointed us as stewards; this means that Catholics believe they have a duty to protect the world and ensure that all people are given the opportunity to share in the world's resources.

Activities

1 Describe what you think the term 'faith in action' means.

Jesus spoke about compassion for those in need. He told his followers the story of the Good Samaritan (Luke 10:25–37); this teaches Catholics that they must see Jesus in everyone they meet and help people who are suffering regardless of their race or religion.

The parable of the sheep and the goats also confirms that we should help others.

'I tell you the truth, whatever you did for one of the least of these brothers of mine, you did for me.' (Matthew 25:40)

The Golden Rule highlights that Christians must treat others as they themselves would wish to be treated. Jesus also said that possessions should not be stored up on Earth where they can be stolen and destroyed, but instead a person should store up riches in Heaven.

 ResultsPlus
Build better answers

Explain why CAFOD works to end world poverty. (8 marks)

 Basic, 1–2-mark answers
Basic answers will just give one or two brief reasons without developing them, or one developed reason.

Good, 3–6-mark answers
Good answers will give up to four brief reasons; one developed and one brief reason; or two developed reasons. Better answers will give either three developed reasons, or a couple of developed reasons along with a couple of brief reasons.

Excellent 7–8-mark answers
Most excellent answers give four developed reasons. Answers that give two fully-developed reasons (which means lots of explanation!) will also reach 7–8 marks. All excellent answers will use some key terms and good English as this is taken into account on (c) questions.

Catholic Social Teaching also reminds us that if we want wealth and possessions this can lead us to envy those who have them while we don't. The tenth Commandment forbids envy.

Catholics believe we should feel compassion (as Jesus did) for those people who are in need. It is unfair for some people not to have their basic human rights, and Catholics believe we should try to find ways of righting those injustices.

How does it help?

CAFOD works with more than 500 partners both overseas and in the UK – all working to reduce poverty overseas. The main ways in which CAFOD does this is by:

Finding a voice for those who are unable to speak out for themselves – CAFOD has been heavily involved with the campaign to drop debt that some poor countries owe. It speaks out on behalf of the poor and helps to promote social justice so that all people are treated with dignity and are able to share in the world's resources.

Education – Poverty is often about lack of access to information and education. CAFOD helps to educate people; this gives developing nations an opportunity to reduce poverty through economic growth and improved education. It also educates people in the UK about the needs of the poor and the work that CAFOD is doing.

Emergency aid – CAFOD provides short-term aid for people who are caught up in disasters and emergencies. This includes blankets, food, medicines, water and shelter. This is not a long-term solution, it is a temporary measure to help people in the aftermath of a disaster.

Long-term aid – CAFOD provides long-term support so that the people can help work themselves out of poverty and so no longer need the help of CAFOD. This could include teaching

them alternative methods of farming so that their crops are able to withstand a drought or providing a well so that a village has clean and safe drinking water. CAFOD helps communities set up small businesses so that they can provide for their families, and the profits go back into the community where they live.

Activities

2 Read one of the Bible passages mentioned on these pages. Explain its teachings. You could also read:
- The rich young man – Mark 10:21–23, or
- Sermon on the mount – Matthew 5–7.

Challenge

3 Design a leaflet or poster advertising the work of CAFOD. Include in it why people should support the work of CAFOD.

CAFOD relies upon fundraising activities to fund its overseas development.

Summary

- CAFOD works to help end world poverty. It seeks to give people dignity and promotes self-sufficiency.
- CAFOD's work is inspired by the Bible and the example of Jesus.

2.11 Matters of life and death in the media

Learning outcomes

By the end of this lesson you should be able to:

- explain how different forms of media tackle matters of life and death
- understand how they reflect a range of different views on life and death issues
- offer your own opinion on how the media deal with these matters and assess how your views may be different from others.

It is important that we see matters that relate to life and death in the media because:

- issues of life and death affect everyone
- people have very strong feelings about these issues
- opinions are very divided and it is important that we know how people think differently
- controversial choices need to be discussed openly
- people have the right to know about developments in these issues
- people need to know how the law may change.

The media use several different ways to present matters to the nation:

- **Newspapers** – They adopt personal opinions and provide interviews with people.
- **Internet** – This can include online newspapers and sites such as the BBC, but anyone can publish on the Internet and it is often not regulated or checked for accuracy.
- **Television news and documentaries** – These offer the opportunity to focus on a major issue at length, identifying different positions on the issue.

- **Soap operas** – These use changing storylines to examine issues in depth in a way that is accessible to the general public.
- **Television dramas** – These are similar to soap operas and some may specifically focus on matters of life and death.
- **Situation comedies** – The main aim of these programmes is to make people laugh, but because they take place in everyday situations and audiences can relate to the characters, these programmes often feature matters of life and death.
- **Films** – These use a detailed plot to examine an issue in depth, often based on a novel that has already introduced this idea to a smaller audience.
- **Cartoons** – Like situation comedies, these may deal with matters of life and death, even those aimed at children.

Activities

1   Look at the television programmes scheduled to be shown this week. How many stories are there about life and death?

2   Select one programme to watch for this next activity. Answer the following questions about the programme, presenting your answers in the form of a spider diagram.

Put the central issue in the middle of the diagram. Then add the different opinions expressed in the programme as the 'legs'. Did the programme writers present all the sides of the argument? Was a religious response to the issue covered? If not, why do you think this was missed out? If it was covered, was it a fair portrayal of religious people's beliefs? Add any other points you think are important.

Soap operas

Soap operas are long-running serials concerned with everyday life in which several storylines are carried over from one episode to the next. Regular events in soap operas include issues of family and relationships, but also issues such as abortion, euthanasia, and dealing with illness and death. There is no one dominant storyline, but several stories are woven together over a limitless number of episodes that focus on how events affect characters, allowing viewers to relate to the events through the familiar characters and think how they may respond themselves.

If a particularly emotional issue has been addressed by a soap, a helpline phone number is often displayed at the end, so people who have been affected by the issues can get support or extra information.

Hollyoaks: *Tina's family mourn the loss of their sister and daughter.*

Activities

3 Do you think people can relate events in soap operas to their lives?

4 Do you think soap operas deal with the after-effects of life and death effectively? Give reasons for and against and use examples from soap operas. Divide your work into three different life and death topics: abortion, death, and suicide or euthanasia.

Films and documentaries

A surprising number of films are made that tackle matters of life and death. In most cases the moral theme of a film is presented alongside the more usual themes of popular film – romance, family dramas, adventures or fantasy – because most films are designed to entertain as well as inform. If the director simply wants to educate the audience about an issue of life or death, they will produce a documentary rather than a feature film.

Activities

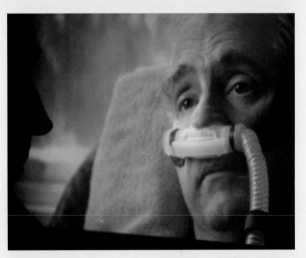

Motor neurone patient, Craig Ewert, was shown on television taking a lethal dose of drugs to end his life.

Challenge

5 Should television shows be allowed to show events such as a person dying? Explain your reasons.

Summary

- A range of media can be used to present matters of life and death to a wide audience.
- Newspapers and television news, soap operas, documentaries and films all take some responsibility for presenting issues to the public.
- Each has different intentions and interests, and some may reflect the opinions of the programme makers or editors while others are more impartial.

examzone

Know Zone
Matters of life and death

Quick quiz

1 Name the three destinations Catholics think are possible after death.

2 What is meant by 'quality of life'?

3 Why might some Christians say that it is wrong to make judgements about quality of life?

4 What is the current UK law on abortion?

5 On what grounds can a woman get an abortion?

6 Why do Catholics oppose abortion?

7 Give three reasons against abortion.

8 Why might some Christians believe that suffering and illness may be valuable?

9 Explain why some countries are poor.

10 Why should Catholics help those who are suffering?

Find out more

For more information on the topics below, go to www.heinemann.co.uk/hotlinks (express code 4219P) and click on the appropriate link.

- Euthanasia
- Poverty
- CAFOD
- Life after death

Plenary activity

Find out about one person who either currently is playing, or in recent history has played, a significant role in shaping the public's opinion on matters of life and death. For example, you could research the life and work of Dan James, Kevin Carter or Diane Pretty who carried out important work campaigning for the right for chronically sick patients to be helped to end their life.

Prepare a presentation on this person for the rest of the class, ensuring that you don't just give facts about them but try to assess how important their case was for publicising such matters and whether you think they had any significant impact on developments in thinking about matters of life and death.

Student tips

Be careful to avoid thinking that all Christians feel the same about issues such as abortion or euthanasia. Sometimes their views differ greatly and they use different writings from the Bible to support them. In (d)-type questions make sure you try to name the branch of Christianity. You can never say 'All Christians believe...' and be absolutely right. The most you can say is that 'Some Christians...' The important thing then is explaining why they think differently – this is the 'because' part of your answer.

Self-evaluation checklist

How well have you understood the topics in this section? In the first column of the table below use the following code to rate your understanding:

Green – I understand this fully

Orange – I am confident I can answer most questions on this

Red – I need to do a lot more work on this topic.

In the second and third columns you need to think about:

- Whether you have an opinion on this topic and could give reasons for that opinion if asked
- Whether you can give the opinion of someone who disagrees with you and give reasons for this alternative opinion.

Content covered	My understanding is red/orange/green	Can I give my opinion?	Can I give an alternative opinion?
Definitions of the key terms and how to use them to answer GCSE questions			
Why Catholics believe in life after death and how this belief affects their lives			
Non-religious belief in life after death (near-death experiences, ghosts, mediums, evidence of reincarnation)			
Why some people do not believe in life after death			
The current law on abortion and why it generates such debate			
The different Christian attitudes to abortion and the reasons for them			
What is meant by euthanasia, the law and the different situations in which it occurs			
Christian attitudes to euthanasia and why people have these opinions			
The causes of world poverty			
How and why CAFOD is trying to end world poverty			
How the media deals with life and death issues and how an issue is presented in the media, including whether the treatment is fair to religious beliefs and religious people			

Introduction

In the exam you will see a choice of two questions on this module. Each question will include four tasks, which test your knowledge, understanding and evaluation of the material covered. A 2-mark question will ask you to define a term; a 4-mark question will ask your opinion on a point of view; an 8-mark question will ask you to explain a particular belief or idea; a 6-mark question will ask for your opinion on a point of view and ask you to consider an alternative point of view.

You have to give your opinion, but make sure you do give two clear and thought-out reasons. These can be ones you have learned in class, even if they are not your own opinion. You mustn't use terms such as 'rubbish' or 'stupid' as these don't show that you are able to think things through carefully.

Again, you can use reasons you have learned from your studies. At this stage you only need to give one point of view, for or against.

Now you have to give the opposite point of view, again using material you have learned during your studies. You don't have to say what you think about these alternative points of view, but you do need to show you understand why they are just as important to consider as your own opinion.

Mini exam paper

(a) What is **non-voluntary euthanasia?** (2 marks)

(b) Do you agree with euthanasia? Give **two** reasons for your point of view. (4 marks)

(c) Explain why some Roman Catholics do not agree with abortion. (8 marks)

(d) 'Your soul will never die.'

In your answer you should refer to Roman Catholic Christianity.

(i) Do you agree? Give reasons for your opinion. (3 marks)

(ii) Give reasons why some people may disagree with you. (3 marks)

Here you need to give a short, accurate definition. You do not need to write more than one clear sentence.

Here you need to explain the reasons why Roman Catholics do not agree with abortion – not simply list arguments against it. This question is worth 8 marks so you must be prepared to spend some time answering it. You will also be assessed on your use of language in this question.

Mark scheme

(a) You can earn **2 marks** for a correct answer, and **1 mark** for a partially correct answer.

(b) To earn up to the full **4 marks** you need to give two reasons (as asked) and to develop them fully. Two brief reasons or only one developed reason will earn **2 marks**.

(c) You can earn **7–8 marks** by giving up to four reasons, but the fewer reasons you give, the more

you must develop them. Because you are being assessed on use of language you also need to take care to express your understanding in a clear style of English, and make some use of specialist vocabulary.

(d) To go beyond **3 marks** for the whole of this question you must refer to Roman Catholicism. The more you are able to develop your reasons the more marks you will earn. Three simple reasons can earn you the same mark as one fully developed reason.

ResultsPlus
Maximise your marks

(c) Explain why some Roman Catholics do not agree with abortion. (8 marks)

Student answer	Examiner comments	Improved student answer
Roman Catholics disagree with abortion because it is against the sanctity of life. This means that life is holy and belongs to God so only God can give life and take it away. They also believe that abortion is murder and is going against one of the Ten Commandments – 'Thou shalt not kill'.	The student gives two important reasons why Roman Catholics are against abortion – sanctity of life and one of the Ten Commandments. These reasons are developed so the student would get four marks. To improve the answer, the student should develop two further reasons or expand on the reasons they have already mentioned.	Roman Catholics disagree with abortion because it is against the sanctity of life. This means that life is holy and belongs to God so only God can give life and take it away. God has a plan for every life and it is wrong for humans to interfere with that plan by taking life away. They also believe that all life beings at conception, so they think that a foetus has the same rights as every other person. Therefore they think of abortion as murder which is against one of God's Ten Commandments 'Thou shalt not kill'. Furthermore Catholics would disagree with abortion because it goes against the teachings of the Church.

Marriage and the family

Introduction

In this section you will learn about the attitudes and beliefs of Christians, and Roman Catholics in particular, towards sex outside marriage, marriage, and divorce. You will consider how attitudes to these topics continue to change. You will learn about Christian attitudes to contraception and homosexuality. You will evaluate the alternative points of view on these topics and come to a personal conclusion with reasons to support it.

Learning outcomes for this section

By the end of this section you should be able to:

- give definitions of the key terms
- outline the changes in attitudes in the UK to marriage, divorce, family life and homosexuality and give reasons for these changes
- describe different Christian attitudes to sex outside marriage, explain why there are different attitudes and express your own point of view with reasons
- explain the purpose of marriage in Roman Catholic Christianity and how this is shown through the marriage ceremony
- describe different Christian attitudes to divorce and reasons for them
- outline Christian attitudes to homosexuality, explain why there are different attitudes and express your own point of view with reasons
- outline the Roman Catholic teachings on family life and its importance
- describe how Roman Catholic parishes help with the upbringing of children and explain how this helps keep the family together
- outline different methods of contraception and explain why they are used
- explain different Christian attitudes to contraception and the reasons for them
- evaluate, with examples, how these issues have been covered in the media.

edexcel ::: key terms

adultery	contraception	nuclear family	promiscuity
civil partnership	faithfulness	pre-marital sex	re-constituted family
cohabitation	homosexuality	procreation	re-marriage

Fascinating fact

Did you know that in 2007 the provisional divorce rate in England and Wales fell to 11.9 divorcing people per 1,000 married population, compared with the 2006 figure of 12.2? The divorce rate was at its lowest level since 1981. Over the same time, fewer people have been getting married. This is due to a number of reasons, including a decline in religious belief.

1 List as many variations of the term 'family' as you can.

2 Look at the images on this page. Which is the odd one out? Give reasons for your answer. Then compare your thoughts with the person sitting next to you.

3 When you think about your own future, do you want to get married? If your answer is yes, what are you hoping for when you get married (for example, to have children, a lifelong arrangement)? If your answer is no, give your reasons and outline what you are hoping for in the future.

4 Do you think attitudes to marriage and family have changed? Give reasons for your answer. Do young people today still hope to have the happy-ever-after of fairy tales? Why or why not?

5 Consider how the media used to present family when films such as *Cinderella* were made in the 1950s. How have things changed? Do you think the media has played a part in the changing attitudes towards sex, marriage, divorce and families?

3.1 Changing attitudes to marriage, divorce, family and homosexuality in the UK (1)

Learning outcomes

By the end of this lesson, you should be able to:

● outline past attitudes to marriage, divorce, the family and homosexuality in the UK

● suggest possible reasons why these attitudes have changed in recent years.

Common attitudes in the past

Marriage

In the past it was expected that most people would get married, and they would usually do this at around the age of 25. It was expected that they would not have a sexual relationship before they got married, not even with the person that they were going to marry.

Divorce

It was assumed that people would not get divorced once they were married. If they did, this would often cause them to fall out with family and friends who would not approve and would have expected the couple to stay together in a bad marriage and 'work it out'.

The family

People were expected not to have children before they married. It was often a big scandal if a girl found herself to be pregnant before she was married. She would definitely be encouraged to marry as soon as she found out about the baby so that the baby would be born 'in wedlock'. Once married, people were expected to have children and stay together to help to raise their family.

edexcel ⠿ key terms

Homosexuality – Sexual attraction to the same sex.

Glossary

Divorce – The legal termination of a marriage.

Marriage – Where a man and a woman are legally united for the purpose of living together as a couple.

Homosexuality

Homosexuality was not accepted at all in the past. People who were homosexual would often hide this and even marry in order to keep up the pretence that they were heterosexual. In Britain in the past, homosexual acts were illegal and people could be arrested and put into prison for engaging in them.

Activities

1 Look at the attitudes from the past described above. Make a list of which ones are the same today and which are different.

Reasons for change

In the UK, attitudes towards marriage, divorce, the family and homosexuality have changed dramatically in recent years. Changes in attitude towards subjects such as these take time. Generally, society has become more accepting of things that have traditionally been considered different and not the 'norm'.

In the film Mona Lisa Smile*, the script writers explored the theme of the role of a woman in the family as times were beginning to change. The film provides lots of examples of how women were expected to stay at home and how things changing caused problems for some people.*

Activities

2 Have you ever had a change of attitude towards something? What caused you to make this change?

The reasons for the changes in attitudes towards marriage, divorce, family and homosexuality could be:

• Historical features such as the abolition of slavery and voting rights for women. Democracy and the right to free speech have also allowed other groups to protest for equal rights in society, and the success of previous campaigns for equality set a standard of acceptance for all groups of people.
• The increasingly global view of the world, through technology, the media and travel. This has enabled people to encounter other attitudes and ways of living different to their own. They are no longer able to say 'this is the right way' because, depending on where you are, different things are accepted by other people who have a different view of the world, and different values and traditions.
• A mixture of cultures and ideas that have come into the UK over past decades as the country has become a multi-faith and multi-ethnic society.

Because groups of people with different traditions and values are living in one place, a consensus of acceptable norms has to be achieved for a harmonious society.

• People are more tolerant of the views of others and accepting of differences. Most of society now celebrates diversity as a positive thing.
• Television has had an impact on the nation. The exploration of issues on programmes such as soap operas, and the presentation of less traditional values as acceptable, gradually encourages people to accept these situations as the norm. For example, in the 1950s the family was represented on television as an all-white family comprising a stay-at-home mother, a working father and two children. This has now been replaced with working mums, mixed-race families and step-parents. The soap opera *Eastenders* has a Muslim family who face the same issues and problems as the other families and are fully accepted on the Square. In *Coronation Street*, a homosexual couple is presented as being completely accepted.

This more tolerant and more accepting attitude to people's differences has in turn reduced the traditional acceptance of Christian teachings and the influence of the Church. The Church has, and is, still deciding on many issues whether to embrace these changes in attitudes or remain bound by biblical principles.

For discussion

Is change always a good thing?

Activities

3 Create a list of things that have changed, but not for the better.

Summary

Attitudes to marriage, divorce, family and homosexuality have changed a great deal in recent years and there are many reasons for this.

3.2 Changing attitudes to marriage, divorce, family and homosexuality in the UK (2)

Learning outcomes

By the end of this lesson, you should be able to:

● understand and give background to the changing attitudes in the UK towards marriage, divorce, family life and homosexuality.

edexcel ⠿ key terms

Civil partnership – A legal ceremony giving a homosexual couple the same legal rights as a husband and wife.

Cohabitation – Living together without being married.

Pre-marital sex – Sex before marriage.

Marriage

Today, there is much more **pre-marital sex** than there was 100 years ago. In 2005, 25 per cent of adults under 60 were cohabiting. **Cohabitation** before marriage is now considered by many people to be not only acceptable but often desirable, in order to 'test out the relationship'. This would not have been the case in the past; it would have been seen as immoral and disgraceful. Marriage rates are the lowest since records began in the 1800s. Today, both men and women expect to be treated equally within the marriage; in the past, it was often the case that the man had the dominant role.

Divorce

There are many more people divorcing today due to a change in the law in 1969. This added 'irretrievable breakdown' to the reasons why a couple could divorce, which made it easier to do so. It also made it much cheaper to divorce, and so it was not only the rich who could divorce but also 'ordinary people'. The divorce rate today stands at 45 per cent of all marriages ending in divorce. In the past, very few people would have had the legal reason, the money or been able to withstand the disapproval of society. Research has suggested that people who cohabit

There are many different types of family in the UK today.

and then go on to marry are more likely to divorce. Maybe one reason that the divorce rates have increased is because there is more cohabitation before marriage. Today, the changing expectations of marriage have led to more people divorcing if marriage is not what they expected it to be. There is also less stigma attached to being divorced.

Family life

It would have been almost unthinkable to have a child outside marriage a hundred years ago; there was often a huge stigma attached to both the child and the parents because of this. Today, this is not the case – children born outside a marital relationship are now a normal part of life and there is no stigma attached. In 2005, 43 per cent of children in the UK were born outside marriage, as opposed to 12 per cent of children in 1980. In the past, it was mostly the role of the woman to raise the children; however, today much more of a responsibility is placed on both parents to raise the children.

Activities

1   Imagine that you have travelled back in time 100 years. How would you explain what attitudes today are like to the people of 100 years ago? What arguments do you think they would give for their way of life as being better than ours?

For discussion

Do you think that the changes to society have led to a better or a worse lifestyle for most people?

Activities

Challenge

2   Carry out your own questionnaire using similar questions about marriage and cohabitation. Are the results the same within your class/year/friends/family?

Homosexuality

Year	The law and how it has changed
Before 1967	Homosexual acts were illegal and the punishment could range from a £5 fine to life imprisonment.
1967	In England and Wales it became legal to engage in homosexual acts provided it was 'in private' and 'with consent'.
1980	In Scotland sex between two men was decriminalised.
1994	The age of consent for two men was lowered from 21 to 18.
2000	The age of consent was lowered to 16 to bring it into line with the age of consent for heterosexual sex.
2001	Homosexual people were legally allowed to register their relationships, giving them the same rights in law as married people. This is called a **civil partnership**; however, many homosexual people prefer to think of it as a 'marriage' ceremony.
2002	Homosexual couples were given the right to adopt a child.

There has never been a law against sexual acts between two women, and therefore there has been nothing to change.

Summary

In this lesson you have learned how attitudes and practice have changed in today's society. You have discovered that we are generally more liberal in our attitudes and more accepting of a variety of different lifestyles.

3.3 Christian attitudes to sex outside marriage

Learning outcomes

By the end of this lesson you should be able to:

- outline the biblical teaching on sex outside marriage
- outline the different attitudes to sex outside marriage in Christianity
- explain why there are different attitudes towards sex outside marriage in Christianity
- evaluate the different points of view about sex outside marriage and give your own opinion with reasons.

The Bible and sexual relationships

The Bible teaches that sex outside marriage is wrong. Sex is an act of love and commitment and should only take place in marriage. This includes having sex before marriage (pre-marital sex) or having sex with someone when you are already married to someone else (**adultery**). Christians are taught to avoid having casual sexual relationships (**promiscuity**) and believe that married couples should show **faithfulness** to each other.

The Bible says:

'You shall not commit adultery.' (Exodus 20:14)

'It is God's will that you should be sanctified: that you should avoid sexual immorality.' (I Thessalonians 4:3)

'But I tell you that anyone who looks at a woman lustfully has already committed adultery with her in his heart.' (Matthew 5:28)

'Do you not know that your body is a temple of the Holy Spirit…' (I Corinthians 6:19)

edexcel ⋮⋮⋮ key terms

Adultery – A sexual act between a married person and someone other than their marriage partner.

Faithfulness – Staying with your marriage partner and having sex only with them.

Promiscuity – Having sex with a number of partners without commitment.

'The wife's body does not belong to her alone, but also to her husband. In the same way, the husband's body does not belong to him alone but also to his wife.' (I Corinthians 7:4)

'The sexual act must take place exclusively within marriage. Outside marriage it always constitutes a grave sin.' (The Catechism of the Catholic Church)

Activities

1 Write down these quotations above and say what you think each of them means. Do you agree or disagree with them? Give reasons.

ResultsPlus
Top tip!

Candidates who give the best answers to questions on this topic remember that 'sex outside marriage' covers both pre-marital and extra-marital sex. Deal with both in your answers.

Roman Catholics say that pre-marital sex is wrong and that sex should only take place within marriage. This is because they recognise sexual intercourse as a gift from God for the married couple. They also say that pre-marital sex is wrong because the Church's teachings and the Catechism state this is the case.

All Christians believe that promiscuity is wrong because it is abusing the gift of sexual intercourse that God has given to married couples. Also, in the Bible it says that your body belongs not to you but to God, and so it should be used in the way that God would want you to use it.

Christians also say that adultery is wrong because it is condemned in the Ten Commandments, and also such action breaks the promise made during the marriage ceremony that the partners would stay faithful to each other.

Liberal views

Other Christians, however, may sometimes take a more liberal view on pre-marital sex. They argue that it is a step on the way to marriage and think that they are showing love by this attitude. Jesus taught that love is important. Some liberal Christians also believe that the Church should update its teachings in line with God-given conscience. They feel that we should use this to make up our own minds about what we consider to be right and wrong. They also argue that the Bible was written so long ago that it cannot apply to our modern society, where life is very different. Churches' views should change to reflect a more modern society.

Still, other Christians argue that we can be deceived by our consciences and make the wrong decisions; therefore, we should follow what Church leaders tell us to follow. Their view is that God's standards do not change. Society may have become more relaxed morally, but that does not mean that God has. Some argue that if the Church continues to change to 'fit in' with modern society, morals will become more and more diluted. The Church's morals may be high, but they give us a standard to live up to.

Activities

2 Create a table or diagram which gives different Christian attitudes to sex outside marriage and the reasons for them.

3 Write a letter to the Catholic Church defending pre-marital sex.

For discussion

Do you think that pre-marital sex should be allowed by the Church? Give arguments for and against.

Summary

In this lesson you have learned about what different groups of Christians say about promiscuity, pre-marital sex and adultery, and how their attitudes are sometimes the same and sometimes different.

3.4 The purposes of marriage in Catholic Christianity and how this is shown in the wedding ceremony

Learning outcomes

By the end of this lesson you should be able to:

● outline the purpose of marriage in Roman Catholic Christianity

● identify the features of a Roman Catholic wedding ceremony and explain how these show the purpose of marriage for a Catholic Christian.

Catholics get married for four main reasons:

1 **Catholic marriage is a sacrament.** A sacrament brings believers closer to God and helps them to get to know him better. It also brings God's blessing on the relationship. In the marriage ceremony, the couple declare their love before God and their family and friends.

2 **Catholic marriage is permanent.** This means that Catholic couples will promise that the marriage will last forever and that they will not divorce. This can be seen in the vows when the couple say '… till death do us part'.

3 **Catholic marriage is exclusive.** This means that the couple will promise that the marriage will be between the couple only and that they will not have a sexual relationship with anybody else. This can be seen when they exchange rings, as they will say 'Take this ring as a sign of my love and fidelity'. Fidelity means faithfulness and so they are promising to keep the marriage exclusive.

4 **Catholic marriage is life-giving.** This means that the couple will promise not only to have children, but also that they will help each other to grow in love, therefore giving 'new life' to each other. This can be seen in the questions in the ceremony, when they are asked 'Will you accept children lovingly from God, and bring them up according to the law of Christ and his Church?' This is a promise of **procreation**.

edexcel ⠿ key terms

Procreation – Making a new life.

Glossary

Sacrament – Outward sign of something holy, it usually is representative of some part of God's relationship with human beings.

Why do you think that this is a good image for a Roman Catholic marriage? What symbol would you draw to demonstrate the meaning of marriage?

Activities

1 Draw three pictures that you believe would 'sum up' a Roman Catholic marriage ceremony and explain them.

Features of a Roman Catholic marriage ceremony

Greeting

The priest will greet the couple and the congregation and will explain to them the meaning of marriage and that it is a sacrament that is permanent, exclusive and life-giving.

Homily and readings

The readings will then take place. These are usually about the nature of marriage and the importance of love. Often the readings that may be used are 1 Corinthians 13 or Ephesians 5:21–33.

Questions

The couple are then asked three questions, to make sure that they understand and intend to keep the marriage permanent, exclusive and faithful:

> N. and N., have you come here freely and without reservation to give yourselves to each other in marriage?
>
> Will you love and honour each other as man and wife for the rest of your lives?
>
> Will you accept children lovingly from God, and bring them up according to the law of Christ and his Church?

Vows

This is the actual moment of the sacrament. It is when the bride gives the sacrament to the groom and the groom gives the sacrament to the bride in these words:

> To have and to hold,
> From this day forward
> For better, for worse,
> For richer, for poorer,
> In sickness and in health,
> To love and to cherish,
> 'Til death us do part.

In the Catholic Church the vow 'to obey' has never been included in the ceremony.

Activities

2 Write your own wedding vows. What do you think are the most important things to include in them?

Challenge

3 Organise and act out your own wedding ceremony within your class.

Acceptance and consent

The priest then accepts the consent of the couple.

> You have declared your consent before the Church. May the Lord in his goodness strengthen your consent and fill you both with his blessings. What God has joined, men must not divide. Amen.

Rings

The rings are then blessed by the priest and exchanged with the words 'Take this ring as a sign of my love and fidelity'.

Blessing

The marriage ceremony then ends with the blessing by the priest in which he will pray that God will make the marriage permanent, exclusive and life-giving.

Signing of the register

This is purely a legal requirement. For this reason it is often done away from the altar, perhaps in the sacristy (behind the altar) of the church.

Activities

4 Complete the chart below.

Part of the ceremony	What happens	How this shows the meaning of a Catholic marriage	Your own symbol for this section
Greeting			
Homily and readings			
Ceremony begins with the questions			
Vows			
Acceptance and consent			
Rings			
Blessing			
Signing of the register			

Summary

In this section you have learned about how Roman Catholic marriage is a sacrament and should be permanent, exclusive and life-giving. Each of these is demonstrated within the marriage ceremony.

3.5 Different Christian attitudes to divorce

Learning outcomes

By the end of this lesson you should be able to:

- outline the different attitudes to divorce
- explain why there are different attitudes towards divorce in Christianity
- evaluate the different points of view about divorce and give your own, with reasons.

A divorce is given by the courts if the marriage is 'irretrievably broken down' (this means that there is no way the couple can ever stay together). Divorce is usually granted because of adultery, unreasonable behaviour or desertion (when one partner leaves the other for a long time).

In the UK about a third of marriages end in divorce and there are about 160,000 divorces each year. People are more inclined to consider getting divorced than they were many years ago, for a number of reasons:

'People are less religious and do not feel bound to their marriage vows.'

'People are less willing to put up with bad treatment from their partner.'

'Divorce is quick and often inexpensive.'

'Divorce does not carry the social stigma that it did in the past.'

Activities

1 Make a list of all the people that you think might get hurt in a divorce.

2 What reasons do you think are given most often when people ask for a divorce?

edexcel ⠿ key terms

Re-marriage – Marrying again after being divorced from a previous marriage.

Different Christian views on divorce

The Roman Catholic Church

Catholic teachings say that in all circumstances divorce is wrong. Roman Catholic couples make a promise in the marriage ceremony to keep their marriage permanent, and this promise should always be kept. Although some Catholics may get a legal divorce, the Roman Catholic Church says that they are still married in the eyes of God and that the sacrament cannot be broken – so they are also still married in the eyes of the Church. Since divorce is not allowed, the Church will also not allow **re-marriage**.

'Anyone who divorces his wife and marries another woman commits adultery against her. And if she divorces her husband and marries another man, she commits adultery.' (Mark 10:11–12)

In some circumstances the Catholic Church will grant an annulment. This is where the Church considers an individual marriage and says that it was never a 'real' marriage to begin with. In such a case the marriage is classed as never having taken place and the people are free then to marry in the Catholic Church.

Some Protestant Churches

Some Protestant Churches permit divorce and will also allow divorced people a re-marriage in church. They do this because they say Christianity teaches that forgiveness is one of the most important things. They feel that if two people have made a mistake in marrying, they should be granted forgiveness for that mistake. Provided that they are sorry for the failure of their last marriage, they should be allowed to remarry within the Church.

Who do you think gets hurt the most when a marriage ends?

Some may also say that marriage is supposed to demonstrate God's love to the world. However, the couple cannot do this if they are continually arguing and miserable. So it may be better for them to divorce than to continue to live in hatred, and in the long run this may be the 'lesser of two evils'. In addition, Jesus allowed divorce in the case of adultery, and so some Christians argue for this reason that divorce should be allowed.

> *'I tell you that anyone who divorces his wife, except for marital unfaithfulness, and marries another woman commits adultery.'* (Matthew 19:9)

Activities

3 Why do you think that the Bible isn't clear on its teachings about divorce?

4 What do you think are the arguments for and against divorce?

ResultsPlus
Build better answers

Do you think divorce is acceptable?
Give **two** reasons for your point of view. (4 marks)

■ **Basic, 1-mark answers**
Basic answers will give their opinion but with just a brief reason.

● **Good, 2–3-mark answers**
These answers will either give two brief reasons (2 marks) or one brief and one developed reason (3 marks) for their opinion.

▲ **Excellent, 4-mark answers**
Answers which receive full marks will give two reasons and develop both of them.

Activities

Challenge

In cases where a member of the family may be in danger due to problems in the marriage, for example from abuse, the Catholic Church will allow the couple to live separately. However, the Church says that neither of them should remarry, as they are still married to their original marriage partner even though they live apart. A person who has divorced and re-married is not allowed to receive Holy Communion.

5 Do you think that the Catholic Church's view is correct where domestic violence and abuse are concerned?

6 Why might the Catholic Church not allow re-married people to receive Holy Communion?

Summary

In this lesson you have learned what the Catholic Church and some Protestant Churches say about divorce and re-marriage, and why they hold differing views.

3.6 Christian attitudes to homosexuality

68

Learning outcomes

By the end of this lesson you should be able to:

● understand different Christian attitudes to homosexuality

● explain why Christians hold different opinions

● express your own opinion and explain why other people have different views.

Attitudes to homosexuality have changed in society in the UK over recent years. The media portrays homosexuality much more widely now, for example in soap operas such as *Coronation Street*. The Church, however, has tended to be more conservative, but a wide range of views are held by Christians.

Different Christian views on homosexuality

Evangelical Protestants

Many Evangelical Protestants believe that all homosexual thoughts and act are wrong and that homosexuals should pray to God to become heterosexual. They believe this because:

● It follows some teachings of the Bible such as: '*No man is to have sexual relations with another man; God hates that.*' (Leviticus 18:22). In the New Testament, Paul writes, '*Neither the sexually immoral… nor homosexual offenders will inherit the Kingdom of God*' (1 Corinthians 6:9–10).

● God created man and woman to be in a marriage relationship together.

● The purposes of sex are to create children and two same-sex partners cannot have a child this way.

● They think that homosexuality is not good for society, as it undermines the family.

Television star John Barrowman has always been openly gay.

Activity

1 Make a list of as many famous homosexual people as you can.

In 2005, singer Elton John entered into a civil partnership with his long-term partner David Furnish. Civil partnerships were a huge step forward in the recognition of homosexual love and commitment in a relationship.

Roman Catholics

The Roman Catholic Church believes that being homosexual is not a sin, but that having homosexual sex is. This is because people cannot help their feelings but people can stop themselves from acting upon them. Therefore they believe that homosexual people should remain celibate (not have sex). This is because:

- The Bible condemns homosexual acts – it does not say that homosexual feelings are a sin.
- Roman Catholics believe sex should only take place within marriage. Any sex which takes place outside of marriage is wrong and as marriage is the uniting of a man and a woman this means that homosexual sex is forbidden.
- They believe that sex is for procreation. Homosexual sex cannot produce children, therefore it is a sexual act that is sinful.

Roman Catholics believe that all forms of discrimination are wrong, including homophobia because the Bible teaches that we are all equal.

Liberal Protestants

Some liberal Christians such as Quakers believe that homosexual feelings and acts are not wrong providing that they occur within a stable relationship. They believe:

- Religion is a spiritual issue not a sexual one.
- The Bible needs to be interpreted to suit today's society and Jesus taught that it was love that mattered the most.
- Same-sex relationships in the Bible were admired in David and Jonathan, and Ruth and Naomi.

The Church of England is divided on its views of homosexuality but generally:

- Homosexual partnerships are judged on the strength of the love and commitment of the partners rather than simply rejecting them as wrong; after all, God created us all in his image.
- It accepts that two people might enter into a homosexual relationship with the hope of enjoying companionship and the expression of love similar to that found in marriage.

ResultsPlus
Top tip!

You can gain higher marks by adding a development to a simple thought or reason in your answer. For example, 'The Roman Catholic Church thinks that homosexuality is wrong, but that homosexual feelings are not. They argue that you cannot change your sexual orientation, but you can control your actions.'

For discussion

What is the difference between marriage and a civil partnership?

Summary

In this lesson you have learned how different groups of Christians view homosexuality and why they argue that they have the correct view.

Activities

2   Copy and fill in the following table:

Who?	Believes what?	Why?
Evangelical Christians		
Roman Catholics		
Liberal Protestants		

3.7 Roman Catholic teachings on family life

Learning outcomes

By the end of this lesson you should be able to:

- outline Roman Catholic teachings on family life
- explain why Roman Catholic Christians hold certain beliefs about relationships within the family
- give your opinion on these beliefs and justify your opinion.

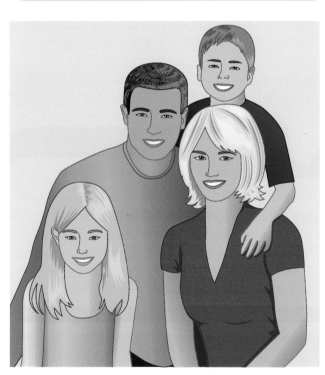

To what extent do you think the nuclear family is the best type of family?

Many Christians believe that the family is the basis for a stable society and it is within the family that children learn about God and the Christian faith. In the UK today the people who make up families, and they way they are made up, has changed from the majority of families being **nuclear families** to other variations such as a **re-constituted families**, extended families, single-parent families and same-sex families.

edexcel key terms

Nuclear family – Mother, father and children living as a unit.

Re-constituted family – Where two sets of children (stepbrothers and stepsisters) become one family when their divorced parents marry each other.

Glossary

Extended family – A family where parents, children and other relations such as grandparents, aunts, uncles and cousins are all living close together.

Single-parent family – One parent living alone with their children as a result of divorce, separation, death or because the parent is unmarried.

Same-sex family – Two same sex parents and their children.

Activities

1 What things do you do to help out at home? What things do your parents do for you?

2 Imagine you have been given the responsibility for writing a set of guidelines for the bringing up of a new baby. What would you include?

Go further than the physical needs of the child. Think about:

- How would you provide for the emotional and spiritual needs of the child?
- How are the values you want to pass on to and nurture in the child best achieved?
- Does the child need a family?
- What purpose does the family serve in the process of nurturing the developing child?

Roman Catholic teaching on family life

Catholics have traditionally believed that people should either decide to get married or become a priest or a nun and remain celibate. If they decide that they want to get married, they have a duty to have children, as they agree to this in the marriage ceremony.

Once they have children, they should raise them as Catholics, which means that they should have them baptised, teach them to pray and about the sacraments, and allow them to attend a Roman Catholic school.

Parents have a duty to love and provide for their children; they should make sure that they are setting them a good example. The children have duties too, to be good, to respect their parents and then to care for them later in life when they may not be able to care for themselves.

Reasons for the Roman Catholic teachings on family life

Roman Catholics believe that the family is very important for the following reasons:

- The family is the best place for children to be raised. They think this because when God made the world He made Adam and Eve and created them as the first family.
- In the Ten Commandments in Exodus 20, children are commanded to 'Honour your father and your mother'.
- Jesus was born into a family that loved and cared for him. Parents today should follow the example of the Holy Family and try to care for their children in the same way.
- In Ephesians 6, St Paul tells us how families should behave and that children should honour their parents and that the parents should care for their children.
- At the marriage service, the couple agree to have children and raise them as Catholics. At baptism they promise to uphold family life.

Activities

3 Do you think that the Catholic teachings on family life are easy to keep? When do you think that somebody may find them hard?

Exam question report

(c) Explain why family life is important in Catholic Christianity. (8 marks) June 2007

How students answered

Most candidates did badly on this question. This was because their answers described religious life generally, rather than explaining why it was important. They also did not refer to Catholic Christianity specifically.

These answers did give some reasons why family life is important to Catholics but did not give enough reasons or develop them to achieve the higher marks.

The few candidates who got excellent marks gave either three simple reasons, two developed reasons or one fully developed reason, and they included things such as Roman Catholic teachings on the importance of the family and the promises about family life made in the marriage and baptism services.

Summary

You have looked at different family groupings and at Roman Catholic teachings on family life. You have considered why Catholics try to keep to these teachings and have thought about your own opinion.

3.8 How Catholic parishes help with the upbringing of children and help to keep the family together

Learning outcomes

By the end of this lesson you should be able to:

- outline how the Roman Catholic Church helps with the upbringing of children
- evaluate and recall how Roman Catholic parishes assist in keeping families together.

Upbringing of children

As discussed on pages 70 and 71, it is generally agreed that raising children is not an easy thing to do and the Church bodies try to offer as much help as they can.

Priests and parishes offer baptism preparation classes and services. There are also Roman Catholic schools that Catholic children can attend and groups that children can go to, such as Sunday schools.

Young people can attend church groups such as Sunday school where Catholic values and teachings are reinforced.

Activities

1 Do you think that the Church has had an influence in helping with your upbringing? If so how?

Keeping the family together

The priests and parishes also work hard with families to help them to stay together. Before a couple marries, they will be taught at the marriage preparation classes about how to help make their marriage work. They will learn about the Catholic teachings that discourage divorce, and this may help them stay together in future.

If they are experiencing problems, the family can get advice from the priest, and there is also a Catholic counselling agency that specialises in marriage.

Do you know what this logo is from? How might this organisation help with the upbringing of children?

Activities

2 Study the diagrams on the next page. Then cover the page and try to redraw the spider diagrams. Check to see how well you have recalled each point.

Baptism

– ensures child becomes part of the Catholic faith

– congregation prays for the family

– family are given God's blessing

– family are given the strength to raise the child as a Catholic

– help of Church community and Godparents

Attending a Catholic school

– teaches ethos of the Catholic faith

– teaches National Curriculum and emphasises shared faith and shared values

Catholic upbringing of children

Sunday school – accessible during Sunday Mass

– for those who find it hard to understand full Mass

– children can worship and learn about their faith at their own level

Church groups

– for all ages

– possibly scouts/guides/brownies/ cubs and rainbow groups

– organised activities to learn about their faith

– youth groups for older children and teenagers

– positive influence in young lives

Helping couples – marriage preparation courses

– help to understand the duties and responsibilities of marriage

– opportunity to see that marriage needs to be worked at and won't always be easy

– a good foundation for their married life

Catholic parishes keeping the family together

Divorce prevention work

– sharing Roman Catholic teaching on divorce

– helping families who are having problems to work harder at their marriage

– helping couples not to give up

– availability of priest:

– for counselling, advice and help

– for guidance on how to strengthen their marriage

– Catholic counselling service called Marriage Care:

– helps families who are experiencing problems in their relationships

– offers advice and help on how to make the marriage work

For discussion

- Do you think that the activities that the Roman Catholic Church runs are useful in helping the family stay together?

- Do you think that a priest is the best person to give marriage advice? Why? Or why not?

Activities

3 Design a Catholic Church newsletter advertising each of the activities that the Church runs to help the family. Don't forget to include a symbol for each of the activities.

Summary

In this lesson you have learned some of the things that Roman Catholic parishes do to try to help with the upbringing of children and how these might help keep the family together.

3.9 Different methods of contraception and reasons people use them

Learning outcomes

By the end of this lesson you should be able to:

- describe different types of contraception
- explain why some people use contraception.

edexcel ::: key terms

Contraception – Intentionally preventing pregnancy from occurring.

What is contraception?

Contraception is the deliberate prevention of pregnancy. There are several methods of artificial contraception:

- the pill – taken daily
- the morning-after pill – taken within 72 hours after unprotected intercourse
- the barrier method, e.g. condoms
- intra-uterine devices (IUDs)
- injection – taken every few months
- sterilisation
- vasectomy.

People who use contraception usually do so because they have decided that it is not appropriate for them to have children. This may be because:

- they want to plan when to have their families and how many children to have
- they consider themselves too young or too old
- they do not believe they would be good parents
- becoming pregnant would be harmful to the health of the mother
- one or both partners carry a genetically inherited condition
- they feel they could not provide financially or emotionally for a child
- they have a lifestyle they feel would not be compatible with having a child
- in the case of a single man, he might not want to be responsible for a woman's pregnancy.

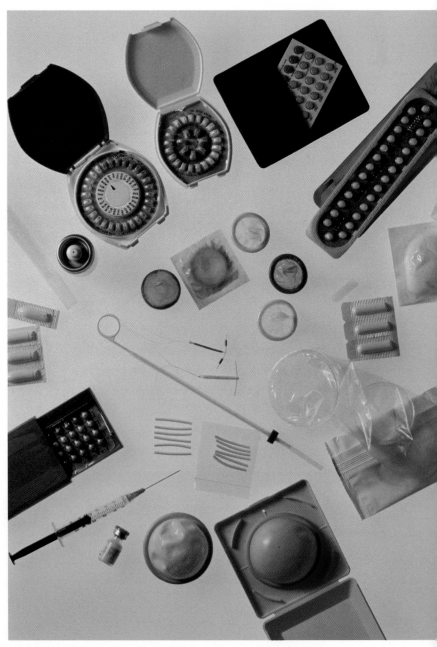

How many of the methods of contraception can you identify?

Specific methods of artificial contraception

Condoms

There are male and female condoms, and they work by forming a barrier to stop the sperm reaching the egg.

The pill

There are many different forms of 'pill' or tablet that a woman can take that will affect her hormones in order to prevent a pregnancy from occurring. As yet, there is no 'pill' that a man can take.

Contraceptive injection/patch/implant

These work in the same way as the pill, but they are given in a different way, e.g. an injection that can last for a number of weeks or a patch that is worn daily. There is also an implant that is placed under the skin and can last for up to three years.

Intra-uterine device (IUD)

This is a small T-shaped plastic device that is placed in the woman's womb by a doctor or nurse. This then stops the sperm and egg meeting or stops the fertilised egg implanting in the womb. It can last between 3 and 10 years.

Diaphragm or cap

This is a flexible rubber dome-shaped device that is placed in the woman's vagina before she has sex and is removed afterwards. It acts as a barrier to stop the sperm reaching the egg.

Sometimes the contraception that has been used may not have worked for some reason, or the couple may have forgotten to use contraception correctly. It is then that 'emergency contraception' may be requested.

This can take two forms. The woman can go to a pharmacy and request the 'morning-after pill', which can be taken within 72 hours of having unprotected sex. It will then either stop an egg being released or not allow the fertilised egg to implant itself in the womb.

The other form of emergency contraception is that an IUD can be inserted up to 120 hours after having unprotected sex. This again will stop an egg being released or not allow the fertilised egg to implant itself in the womb.

Activities

For more information about contraceptive devices, go to www.heinemann.co.uk/hotlinks (express code 4219P) and click on the appropriate link.

1   Research the different types of contraception available.

2   Choose one type of contraception and explain what some people might argue are the benefits and problems with using this type of contraception.

Family planning

A natural method of family planning, favoured by Catholics, is the 'rhythm method', which means planning sexual intercourse around the woman's menstrual cycle to avoid her fertile time.

For discussion

Do you think that contraception helps to improve the quality of people's lives?

Summary

In this lesson you have learned about a variety of contraceptive devices and how they work to prevent a baby developing.

3.10 Christian attitudes to contraception

Learning outcomes

By the end of this lesson you should be able to:

- explain different Christian attitudes towards contraception
- explain why they hold different attitudes
- give your opinion on these different attitudes
- understand why some people may have different views.

Activities

1 Explain the reasons why Christians disagree on contraception.

2 'It is better to use contraception than to have an unwanted baby.' Do you agree? Give reasons for your view.

Different Christian opinions

Many people use contraception at some point in their lives, but some religious believers are opposed to artificial contraception.

Who	Believe what	Why
Roman Catholic Christians and conservative Evangelicals	Every sexual act should be open to the possibility of conception	• Using artificial methods of contraception is wrong because they prevent humans from fulfilling God's command *'be fruitful and multiply'* (Genesis 1:28). • Sex was given by God for procreation and so every sexual act should allow for the possibility of conception taking place. • Contraception has encouraged promiscuity and the spread of sexually transmitted diseases. • The purpose of marriage is to have children. • These views have been upheld and reaffirmed by popes.
The Church of England and more liberal Christians	Do not regard contraception as against God's plan	• The essence of Christianity is love, and contraception can be used to protect a woman's health. • Reducing the size of families gives children a better standard of living. • God created sex for pleasure and to provide an experience unique to the married couple; contraception allows the sex to be free from fear of pregnancy and provides the couple with safe pleasure. • There is nothing in the Bible that says contraception is wrong.

Can contraception be viewed as abortion?

The way the contraceptive device stops pregnancy is a concern for some Christians. For most (although not Catholics), a barrier method such as the cap or condom is acceptable. This is because the sperm and egg are prevented from meeting and so conception cannot take place. The conventional pill, which prevents conception, is also acceptable to some Christians.

However, the coil and the morning-after pill (which act after conception, and prevent implantation of the egg in the womb) are considered by some Christians to be equivalent to an abortion and therefore unacceptable.

Activities

3 Say whether the following statements are TRUE or FALSE.

(a) The Roman Catholic Church does not agree with any form of artificial contraception. They believe that sex within marriage should be open to creating new life.

(b) Most other Christians say that contraception should not be used by married couples.

(c) Catholics agree with contraception being used outside marriage.

(d) Catholics disagree with the use of contraception within marriage. They argue that it is interfering with God's plan for procreation. They will, however, permit the couple to use 'natural family planning'.

(e) Natural family planning is where the couple, in conjunction with a doctor, work out when the woman is fertile each month, and abstain from sex during these times. This method can also be used in reverse if the couple are actively trying to have a baby.

(f) Most other Christians allow contraception to be used if it is to limit family size or to improve the woman's health. In 1930 the Lambeth conference said that it was permissible for members of the Church of England to use contraception if there was an 'ethically acceptable reason' for the couple not to have children.

(g) The Bible makes a clear statement about the use of contraception.

sex, a person could die of Aids. Some Catholics are now looking again at this issue for this reason.

For more information about views on contraception, go to www.heinemann.co.uk/hotlinks (express code 4219P) and click on the appropriate link.

ResultsPlus
Build better answers

'Contraception makes casual sex acceptable.' In your answers you should refer to Roman Catholic Christianity.

(i) Do you agree? Give reasons for your opinion. (3 marks)

(ii) Give reasons why some people may disagree with you. (3 marks)

■ **Basic, 1-mark answers**
Basic answers to both parts of the question will give just one simple reason for their opinion and one simple reason for the opposite point of view.

● **Good, 2-mark answers**
Answers will receive two marks for two simple reasons or one developed reason. Therefore if they do this for both their own opinion and the opposite point of view, they will get four marks in total. However, if the answer to both parts of the question does not include the Roman Catholic view, then students cannot get more than three marks in total.

▲ **Excellent, 3-mark answers**
Excellent answers will give three simple reasons, two developed reasons or one fully developed reason. If they do this for their own opinion and the opposite point of view they will get six marks in total.

Contraception and sexually transmitted diseases

The use of contraception to protect against sexually transmitted diseases is one of the strongest arguments for its use, because sex in today's society poses a greater threat to people than pregnancy. From just one act of unprotected

Summary

Most Christians today, although not Catholics, accept some form of contraception as a responsible way of planning a family. Most will also see children as a blessing from God, but will allow that this does not mean having an unlimited number of children.

Answers: (a) true (b) false (c) false (d) true (e) true (f) true (g) false.

3.11 Media and marriage and family

Family in the media

Often in the media, marriage and stable family life are not seen as something that is important. Instead, marriage is portrayed trivially and as something that can be ended quickly with few consequences. This can be demonstrated by a Birmingham radio station that held a competition called *Two strangers and a wedding* in which people were invited to compete in order to win the chance to marry a complete stranger. The first time this competition took place, the couple separated three months later. The second time the competition took place, the audience were given an Internet vote about who should marry.

The majority of the families that we see in the soaps are not the traditional nuclear family with children. Many of the families are portrayed as having suffered domestic violence. Adultery is also committed and various other factors join to make the family unable to continue and they end up separating. Rarely do we see a family struggling to make the marriage work or the effects that a divorce can have upon the children.

Children in the media

Children, often teenagers, are portrayed in the media as unruly and unwilling to listen to their parents. They may be seen on the television as

Who is this family? Has the media portrayed them in a positive light?

answering back to their parents and being disobedient. We rarely see a child who is willing to study hard, gain good exam results and then go on to be a successful adult – although this is how the majority of children behave. This type of upbringing does not make for the most entertaining television. Rather, we are more likely to see an abused and neglected child who is unloved and uncared for by their parents, and again this is not the reality of many households in Britain today.

Activities

1 Name as many different families that appear in the media as you can. (You can include soap operas, radio programmes, television comedies, etc.)

2 Categorise these families depending on what type of family they are, e.g. nuclear, single-parent, extended, etc. What do you notice from doing this exercise?

These images of marriage and the family convince us that an 'ordinary' family is the exception; that parents are often committing adultery and fighting and arguing, when in reality many families experience peaceful lives together.

Children are given the idea that other people their ages are constantly fighting with their parents, being neglected and abused and generally struggling to survive. Again, this is often not the case. Many children who have poor lives at home are able to get help from various sources, but this is often not shown. Nevertheless, sometimes programmes will put a helpline at the end of the show, which may help families that are suffering distress.

Focusing on one issue of marriage and family life and one form of the media:

- Choose one issue, say, 'sex outside marriage' (you could choose one of the other issues if you wish).
- Ask yourself how the media handles this issue. In the main, sex before marriage is now represented in the soaps as the normal thing to do. It is expected that the characters will have sex before marriage and no one seems to be concerned about casual sex (promiscuity).

- Ask yourself how the Christian view is handled by the media. In the storylines, the Christian attitude is rarely represented, or if it is, the Christian character is often portrayed as someone who is not familiar with modern values and attitudes towards sex. Do you think that this is fair?

What you need to do for the exam

It is important to learn to look for things in storylines that are going to help you answer the examination questions.

- Watch the programme carefully; identify an issue that is covered.
- Look at the information about this issue from when you studied it. Identify what the different attitudes towards this issue are, including the non-religious ones.
- Now, watching the different characters in the storyline, identify which attitude they are representing. This is how the issue is being dealt with, explored through the characters and their points of view.
- Which attitudes were not covered?
- How could this storyline have been improved to cover all the different points of view?
- If the Christian point of view was covered, do you think the way the religious attitude was presented was fair to Christians?
- If the Christian attitude was not covered, how could it have been added?

Activities

3 Do the above exercise for a soap, a film and a newspaper report.

4 Evaluate how one issue of marriage and family life is presented in one form of the media. Consider the evidence as to whether coverage of this issue is fair to religious people.

Summary

The media portray many issues surrounding marriage and family life.

examzone

Know Zone
Marriage and the family

Quick quiz

1 What word means making a promise before God in a wedding ceremony?

2 What is 'adultery'?

3 Suggest a social reason why a couple might cohabit.

4 Name two forms of artificial contraception.

5 What are the purposes of Roman Catholic marriage?

6 Why do Catholics oppose divorce?

7 Why does the Bible highlight the importance of the family?

8 How do Catholic parishes help families?

9 Why might Christians be against the use of contraception?

10 Name a soap opera storyline you could use in the exam for the 'Marriage and family' section.

Plenary activity

Create ideas maps for each of the topics within this section. Remember to include:

- any 'facts' or laws that you need to know
- arguments for and against each issue
- Catholic teachings on the issue
- different Christian opinions
- your own opinion with reasons.

Find out more

For more information on the topics below, go to www.heinemann.co.uk/hotlinks (express code 4219P) and click on the appropriate links.

- Roman Catholic views
- Christian views

Student tips

When I studied GCSE Religious Studies I found this unit the hardest to appreciate as I felt that it presented a wrong picture of marriage and family in society today. It just wasn't realistic because no one I know is in a religious family and the attitudes of some religious people to issues such as homosexuality are, I think, unacceptable. It wasn't until I visited one of my friends, who is a Christian, that I saw that some people do take religion seriously and it does influence the way they live. It wouldn't suit me, but it made me understand that there are good reasons for some people to live that way.

Self-evaluation checklist

How well have you understood the topics in this section? In the first column of the table below use the following code to rate your understanding:

Green – I understand this fully

Orange – I am confident I can answer most questions on this

Red – I need to do a lot more work on this topic.

In the second and third columns you need to think about:

- Whether you have an opinion on this topic and could give reasons for that opinion if asked
- Whether you can give the opinion of someone who disagrees with you and give reasons for this alternative opinion.

Content covered	My understanding is red/orange/green	Can I give my opinion?	Can I give an alternative opinion?
Changing attitudes to marriage, divorce, family life and homosexuality in the United Kingdom and the reasons for them			
Christian and Catholic attitudes to sex outside marriage and the reasons for them			
The purposes of a Catholic marriage			
The features of the Catholic wedding ceremony and how this shows the purposes of marriage			
Different Christian and Catholic attitudes to divorce, and the reasons for them			
Different Christian and Catholic attitudes to homosexuality, and the reasons for them			
Christian and Catholic teachings on family life and its importance			
How Catholic churches help with the raising of children and keeping families together			
Different Christian and Catholic attitudes to contraception, and the reasons for them			
How the media present issues about marriage and family and whether their portrayal is fair to Christians			

Introduction

In the exam you will see a choice of two questions on this module. Each question will include four tasks, which test your knowledge, understanding and evaluation of the material covered. A 2-mark question will ask you to define a term; a 4-mark question will ask your opinion on a point of view; an 8-mark question will ask you to explain a particular belief or idea; a 6-mark question will ask for your opinion on a point of view and ask you to consider an alternative point of view.

You must give your opinion, but make sure you do give two clear and thought-out reasons. These can be ones you have learned in class, even if they are not your own opinion. You mustn't use terms such as 'rubbish' or 'stupid' as these don't show that you are able to think things through carefully.

Now you have to give the opposite point of view, again using material you have learned during your studies. You don't have to say what you think about these alternative points of view, but you do need to show you understand why they are just as important to consider as your own opinion.

Mini exam paper

(a) What is **cohabitation**?
     (2 marks)

(b) Do you think divorce is better than an unhappy marriage?

     Give **two** reasons for your point of view. (4 marks)

(c) Explain why family life is important for Roman Catholics. (8 marks)

(d) 'No Christian should be homosexual.'

     In your answer you should refer to Roman Catholic Christianity.

     (i)   Do you agree? Give reasons for your opinion. (3 marks)

     (ii) Give reasons why some people may disagree with you. (3 marks)

Here you need to give a short, accurate definition. You do not need to write more than one clear sentence.

Here you need to explain the reasons why family life is important for Roman Catholics and not simply list general reasons. This question is worth 8 marks so you must be prepared to spend some time answering it. You will also be assessed on your use of language in this question.

Again, you can use reasons you have learned from your studies. At this stage you only need to give one point of view, for or against.

Mark scheme

(a) You will earn **2 marks** for a correct answer, and **1 mark** for a partially correct answer.

(b) To earn up to the full **4 marks** you need to give two reasons (as asked) and to develop them fully. Two brief reasons or only one developed reason will earn **2 marks**.

(c) You can earn **7–8 marks** by giving up to four reasons, but the fewer reasons you give, the more

you must develop them. Because you are being assessed on use of language, you also need to take care to express your understanding in a clear style of English, and make some use of specialist vocabulary.

(d) To go beyond **3 marks** for the whole of this question you must refer to Roman Catholicism. The more you are able to develop your reasons, the more marks you will earn. Three simple reasons can earn you the same mark as one fully developed reason.

ResultsPlus
Maximise your marks

(d) 'No Christian should be homosexual.'
In your answer you should refer to Roman Catholic Christianity.
(i) Do you agree? Give reasons for your opinion. (3 marks)
(ii) Give reasons why some people may disagree with you. (3 marks)

Student answer	Examiner comments	Improved student answer
(i) I disagree with the claim that no Christian should be homosexual because this is an unloving approach. Some people will be homosexual because they are naturally that way and there is no point using religious teaching against them as that is unkind.	The candidate has clearly given their opinion and a reason for it. This will gain two marks as the candidate has only developed one idea.	(i) I disagree with the claim that no Christian should be homosexual because this is an unloving approach. Many liberal Christians would agree with me that people are homosexual because they are naturally that way and there is no point using religious teaching against them as that is unkind. There are homosexual Christians who believe that God has created them that way.
(ii) Some people may disagree because they do not believe that homosexuality is natural and that if the teachings of Christianity are against it, they must obey those teachings, whether it feels right for them or not.	This answer is very simple and does not describe the religious teachings that are mentioned and why they may be used by some believers to take the opposite view.	(ii) Some people may disagree with me because it says in the Bible that homosexuality is a sin. These Christians do not believe that homosexuality is natural. Some Christians believe that sex should always be within marriage and is for having children, and because homosexuals cannot get married or conceive children together, it is not right.

Religion and community cohesion

Introduction

In this section you will investigate how the roles of men and women have changed. You will also learn how religion affects people's attitudes towards other faiths and the community. In addition you will look at how the Roman Catholic Church helps promote racial harmony and community cohesion.

Learning outcomes for this section

By the end of this section you should be able to:

- give definitions and examples of key terms
- describe the changing attitudes towards gender roles in the UK
- explain the different Christian attitudes to equal rights for women in religion
- understand how the UK works as a multi-ethnic society (discrimination, racism)
- understand the current legislation and the action of the government to promote community cohesion
- explain how and why the Roman Catholic Church helps asylum seekers and immigrant workers in the UK
- explain why Roman Catholics feel they should help promote racial harmony
- outline the different Christian attitudes to other religions (exclusivism, inclusivism, pluralism)
- understand how the UK works as a multi-faith society
- evaluate the issues that are raised for religion by a multi-faith society
- describe the ways in which religions work to promote community cohesion in the UK
- explain how religion and the community have been portrayed in one form of the media.

edexcel ::: key terms

community cohesion	interfaith marriages	prejudice	religious freedom
discrimination	multi-ethnic society	racial harmony	religious pluralism
ethnic minority	multi-faith society	racism	sexism

Fascinating fact

In the 2001 UK Census, ethnic minorities made up 9 per cent of the total population of England compared with only 2 per cent in both Scotland and Wales and less than 1 per cent in Northern Ireland. For more information about the ethnic make-up of the UK, go to www.heinemann.co.uk/hotlinks (express code 4219P) and click on the link for national statistics (ethnicity).

1 Other than Christianity, what other religions exist in the UK? Which can you recognise in the image?

2 Why do you think it is important for religions to work together? Discuss an issue they might work together on.

3 Can you think of any examples of conflict in communities of the UK that have made the news in the past?

4.1 Changing attitudes to gender roles in the UK (1)

86

edexcel key terms

Discrimination – Treating people less favourably because of their ethnicity/gender/colour/sexuality/age/class.

Prejudice – Believing some people are inferior or superior without even knowing them.

Sexism – Discriminating against people because of their gender (being male or female).

A woman's role?

Activities

1   **(a)** Look at the different images of women. Which is the odd one out and why?

   (b) Put the pictures into an order showing how you think women's roles have changed over the years. What makes you think they have changed? What has changed? Are women now equal to men?

Sexism and the role of women

Sexism is a form of **prejudice** and means treating people unfairly because of their gender. Women have felt that they have suffered prejudice and **discrimination** simply due to the fact that they are female. Women were not allowed the right to vote until 1918, and even then the vote was only given to women of age 30 and older – whereas all men age 21 and older could vote.

Women had few job opportunities. The majority worked in domestic service, shops or textile mills. If men and women did the same work, women were paid less than men. Women were not given the same opportunities for promotion, as it was believed that they could not perform tasks as efficiently as men, or that they would leave work to raise a family.

has changed as well. Many men now share equally in the running of a household and childcare. Men are also entitled to paternity leave (time off) when their partner gives birth. The increased financial pressure on families has also led to the creation of a 'househusband' where it is the man who stays at home and looks after the home and children, while the woman goes to work.

Why gender roles have changed

Two world wars, the introduction of the contraceptive pill, increased mechanisation and technology, and a political campaign over a woman's right to work have all contributed to a change in attitudes towards gender roles. Women now have much broader opportunities to work than those of previous generations. Nevertheless, despite changes in the law, there are still instances where gender is discriminated against in employment and in other areas of life. Changing deep-rooted prejudice can be very hard and takes a long time.

Activities

2 Make a list of some of the possible causes of prejudice against women.

3 Are there any ways in which men are seen as inferior to women?

4 What jobs and roles do you think are traditionally male or female? Make a table like the one below and see what jobs you can think of.

Traditional men's roles	Traditional women's roles
Earning money	Looking after the children
DIY	Ironing

Changing gender roles in twenty-first century Britain

In the twenty-first century, women are no longer willing to be treated differently from men. Women now lead very different lives from the ones they once did. They have equal access to education and voting, and the law is designed to protect women from being discriminated against.

It is not just the role of women that has changed. The traditional view of a man's role and function

Activities

5 Why do you think the roles of men and women have changed? Discuss ideas to form a spider diagram or ideas map of reasons.

6 Job titles have changed. We no longer say 'fireman' but use the term 'fire fighter'. Make a list of any terms or job titles that might still be regarded as sexist.

Summary

In this lesson you have learned how and why attitudes to the roles of men and women have changed in the UK.

4.2 Changing attitudes to gender roles in the UK (2)

Learning outcomes

By the end of this lesson you will be able to:

- outline a brief history of women's rights
- explain how the laws on gender equality have changed in the UK
- evaluate whether you think these laws have been effective.

A brief history of women's rights

In 1897, Millicent Fawcett founded the National Union of Women's Suffrage in order to gain the vote and increased equality for women. 'Suffrage' means the right to vote and that is what women wanted.

Millicent Fawcett believed in peaceful protest. She argued that:

- while women could hold responsible posts in society such as sitting on school boards, they were not trusted to vote
- if Parliament made laws and if women had to obey those laws, then women should be part of the process of making those laws
- if women paid taxes as men did, they should have the same rights as men.

However, despite her protests there was very slow progress.

In 1903, Emmeline Pankhurst founded the Suffragettes. Women were no longer prepared to wait for the right to vote. They were prepared to use any method possible to secure 'Votes for Women'. In 1913 the Suffragettes had their first 'martyr'. Emily Wilding Davison threw herself under the king's horse at the Derby Epsom Race Course and died four days later due to her injuries.

Eventually, women secured the right to vote. This marked a turning point for women's rights. The demands made by two world wars meant that women had to go out to work. This work included traditional male jobs such as land work and factory roles. When the Second World War had ended, women did not want to return to their traditional lives of cooking and caring – working had given them both personal and financial freedom. Women campaigned for the right to be able to continue to work. The feminist movement in the 1960s then began to challenge the stereotyped image of women.

Activities

1 Look back over the brief history of women's rights and make a note of what you consider to be the most significant events that brought about a change in attitudes to women's roles.

2 Some claim that Emily Davison's actions probably did more harm than good to the cause as she was a highly educated woman. Many men asked the simple question – if this is what an educated woman does, what might a less well-educated woman do? How can they possibly be given the right to vote? Write arguments for and against this statement.

ResultsPlus
Watch out!

Some candidates focus on revising the history of women's rights. This is important, but it is equally important to revise what inequalities remain today, as you may be asked about either topic in the exam.

Women still campaign for equal rights today.

Equality legislation

Growing pressure from feminists resulted in the passage of important acts that aimed to give women equal rights to those of men.

- The Equal Pay Act 1970 states that women are to be paid the same as men who do the same or broadly similar jobs.
- The Sex Discrimination Act 1975 makes it illegal to suggest in an advertisement for a job that it is only for men, or only for women. Women and men must be given equal opportunities for promotion within the workplace.
- The Employment Protection Act 1996 makes it illegal to dismiss a woman because she is pregnant. It allows every woman maternity leave if she wants it.

Remaining inequalities today

There has been a gradual closing of the wage gap between men and women since 1975. However, there is still a noticeable gap, and in addition women are not achieving promotion in equal numbers to men. Often discrimination has been suggested as a major reason for these differences in earnings and promotion. Others have suggested that women choose certain occupations that are deemed as 'female' so that they can balance work and family obligations.

Activities

3 Despite the changes in legislation, there are far fewer women in top jobs than men. Why do you think this is the case?

The role and view of women has also altered due to changes in women's lifestyle and opportunity of choice. The development of the contraceptive pill allowed many women to choose when to have a child. There are more examples of successful women portrayed in the media for their achievements in sport and music. Many women feel that they do have equal rights and have been given the same opportunities as men, while some still believe that career breaks to have children and sexist attitudes mean they have to work twice as hard as their male colleagues to achieve success.

Kelly Holmes winning gold at the 2004 Olympics.

Activities

Challenge

4 Examine how the media portrays women; compare the fact to the fiction, for example, news coverage of real-life women to soap opera characters played by women.

Summary

The Suffragettes and the world wars began the movements for women's rights. The government created laws designed to protect and ensure equality for women. Society is evolving and with it the view of traditional roles. Discrimination on the grounds of gender is no longer permitted.

4.3 The different Christian attitudes to equal rights for women in religion and the reasons for them

Learning outcomes

By the end of this lesson you should be able to:

● understand and explain the different Christian attitudes towards the roles of men and women in religion

● describe the different opinions regarding the ordination of women.

Jesus's attitude towards women

Jesus was born into a society where women had a second-class role. Their husbands owned them. In a public place, a man would not acknowledge a woman, even his wife or daughter.

Jesus's treatment of women contrasted with the accepted attitudes of the time. He always treated women with great respect. Jesus had many women followers whom he taught and prayed with. The Bible tells of several incidents where Jesus showed that he believed women were equal to men.

What message was Jesus sending out by having women followers?

The women who followed Jesus supported him by watching as he was crucified. They went to anoint his body and discovered that Jesus had risen from the dead. One of the first people to see Jesus after the resurrection was Mary Magdalene.

Activities

1 The picture shows Mary supporting Jesus. Why do you think he did not choose women disciples?

2 (a) Read the story of the anointing of Jesus at Bethany (Mark 14:3–9). Then, in your own words, outline the incident of the anointing of Jesus. Why did Jesus say that the woman's action would be *'Preached throughout the world'*?

(b) What do you think this incident teaches about the role of women in Christianity?

The Bible and gender roles

Many people claim that the Bible sends out mixed messages about the role of women. Although Jesus treated women as his equal and encouraged others to do the same, some would argue that he never took this a stage further and made them disciples, and the teachings in the Bible suggest that men are of greater importance.

Activities

3 Use a Bible to look up and discuss the Bible references on the next page. Take a large piece of paper and in pairs use the Bible references to fit them on the correct side of the scale – one side supporting equality and the other supporting the view that men are superior to women.

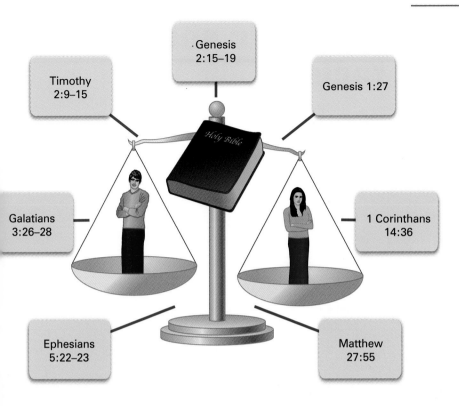

Different Christian attitudes towards the ordination of women

Among Christians today there are differences in the role of women in the Church. In 1994 the Church of England decided to allow the ordination of women priests. Not everyone agreed, and as a consequence some believers left the Church of England and many joined the Catholic Church.

The Church of England and other modern, liberal Protestants allow women to be priests because:

- St Paul wrote that in Christ there is neither male nor female.
- of the actions of Jesus towards women in the Gospels.
- of the possible existence of female priests in the early Church.
- the Gospels were written at a time when women were treated differently, and the Church needs to evolve and change with the rest of society.

The Catholic Church does not ordain women as priests. It believes that men and women are equal and have equal

status in society. Women are allowed to teach and study theology. They can be Eucharistic ministers and lectors, but they cannot be ordained as priests. The Church bases this decision on the following evidence:

- Jesus was a man, and a priest has the authority of representing Jesus at Mass.
- All of Jesus's apostles were men and apostolic succession proceeds through the bishops, who are all male.
- The Catechism teaches that men and women are equal but that only men can be priests.

Traditional Evangelical Protestants believe that men and women have different and very separate roles. Women in these Churches are not permitted to join the ministry or speak in the services. Their evidence is based on:

- St Paul's teaching in 1 Timothy that women should be silent in Church.
- Christ having authority over the Church as a husband has authority over his wife.
- Jesus never had any female apostles and made no exception to this rule, not even for his mother, Mary.

Activities

4 Explain in your own words the reasons why the Catholic Church does not ordain women priests.

Summary

Catholic Christians believe that men and women are equal but that only men can be priests as they represent Jesus at the Mass. Liberal Protestants believe women have equal roles and allow them to be ordained. Traditional Protestants believe that men and women have different roles and women should not be ordained or speak in the Church.

4.4 The UK as a multi-ethnic society – discrimination and racism

Learning outcomes

By the end of this lesson you should be able to:

- explain what is meant by a multi-ethnic society
- outline background and benefits to the UK of being a multi-ethnic society
- understand the problems caused by racism and discrimination.

edexcel ⠿ key terms

Ethnic minority – A member of an ethnic group (race) that is much smaller than the majority group.

Multi-ethnic society – Many different races and cultures living together in one society.

Racial harmony – Different races/colours living together happily.

Racism – The belief that some races are superior to others.

The United Kingdom has always been made up of people from other lands, such as the Celts, Romans, Vikings and Normans. Persecuted peoples have sought refuge here, such as the Huguenots (17th-century French Protestants), Jews during Hitler's regime in Europe and many Eastern Europeans after the Second World War. This background has reinforced the nation's policy on respecting the human freedom and dignity of each person within it.

Soldiers from all over the Empire fought for Britain in the Second World War.

During the Second World War over two million soldiers from the British Empire fought for Britain and many came to Britain during these years. After the war, citizens of the British Empire were allowed to settle in the UK. They brought with them their skills, customs and families. They helped to lessen the labour shortage created by the loss of life in the war. Immigration continues today.

Activities

1 Detail what factors influence people in their decision to enter the UK.

2 Discuss with the person next to you what you think would be an immigrant's first impression of the UK on arrival after the Second World War.

According to the Economic & Social Research Council, in the 2001 Census, '92.1 per cent of the UK population described themselves as white… The remaining 7 per cent (4.6 million) belonged to non-white ethnic minority groups'. This represents 'a 53 per cent growth in the minority ethnic population between 1991 and 2001'. Of this percentage, '45 per cent of the UK's entire minority ethnic population lives in London'.

Having many different races and nationalities brings diversity to a country. The UK can be said to be a much more interesting place because of its diversity, with different foods, clothing, music and films. Living in a **multi-ethnic society** can help to break down stereotypes, and it enables people to recognise the similarities that unite people as human beings.

	Count	Total population %	Minority ethnic population %
White	54,153,898	92.1	n/a
Mixed	677,117	1.2	14.6
Asian or Asian British			
Indian	1,053411	1.8	22.7
Pakistani	747,285	1.3	16.1
Bangladeshi	283,063	0.5	6.1
Other Asian	247,664	0.4	5.3
Black or Black British			
Black Caribbean	565,876	1.0	12.2
Black African	485,277	0.8	10.5
Black other	97,585	0.2	2.1
Chinese	247,403	0.4	5.3
Other	230,615	0.4	5.0
All minority ethnic population	4,635,296	7.9	100
All population	58,789,194	100	n/a

ESRC, 'Ethnic Minorities in the UK'.

Problems of racism and discrimination

Issues of **racism** are not new. Although slavery was abolished 200 years ago, many people from **ethnic minorities** still encounter unfair treatment in this country, often where their families have lived for generations. Racism extends beyond just judging a person based on the colour of their skin – it involves treating them differently and discriminating against them because of their race.

Racism can create tension, violence and division in a community. It also prevents people from playing a full and active role in society. Many people from ethnic minorities feel that they are denied access to jobs and opportunities simply because of their ethnic origin. Although in the UK discrimination has been made illegal by a number of Acts of Parliament, it is easier to legislate against discrimination than it is to change deeply rooted prejudices in order to achieve **racial harmony**.

ResultsPlus
Exam question report

What is a multi-ethnic society? (2 marks) June 2007

How students answered

Many of the candidates who received 0 marks for this question got confused and defined 'multi-faith' instead of 'multi-ethnic' society.

Most of the candidates who scored 1 mark for this question gave the response that a multi-ethnic society is a mixture of different people.

Most candidates wrote excellent answers that explained that a multi-ethnic society is one made up of different races and different cultures.

Activities

3 Do you think there are more advantages or disadvantages to living in a multi-ethnic society? Give reasons for your answer.

Challenge

4 Find out information concerning the murder of Stephen Lawrence. What do you think this incident tells us about racism in the UK? For more information about the murder of Stephen Lawrence, go to www.heinemann.co.uk/ hotlinks (express code 4219P) and click on the appropriate link.

Summary

The UK has always been a multi-ethnic society. A multi-ethnic society encourages change, harmony and diversity among different peoples, but some groups still feel marginalised and unwelcome.

4.5 Government action to promote community cohesion

94

edexcel ⠿ key terms

Community cohesion – A common vision and shared sense of belonging for all groups in society.

What is community cohesion?

Community cohesion is a government strategy. It involves different communities (such as schools, Churches, youth groups, community groups) living and working together and having a shared vision for their future together. The government has outlined four aims that these communities should have in common:

● shared vision and a sense of belonging

● appreciation and valuing of the differences between people

● availability of equal opportunities for all in the community

● strong and positive relationships that continue to be developed in the workplace, in schools and in the wider community.

The government has put in place various measures and legislation to promote community cohesion and to try to prevent prejudice and discrimination.

Activities

1 What factors do you think would encourage a person to want to move their life and family to the UK?

2 Why do you think some white people in the UK fear the rise in immigrants moving to the UK?

3 Two of the views expressed in the cartoon on this page do not promote community cohesion – what are the consequences of attitudes such as these? Make a table like the one below and complete it with your thoughts.

Racial discrimination can result in many immigrants…
… living in poor areas as people don't want them in their community

'I don't mind people from abroad but I don't like any of their foreign food and think they are taking all our jobs.'

'I don't understand why they wear different clothes; why can't they dress in English clothes and eat British food?'

'I really enjoy learning about where my friends lived and I have even been to the temple.'

Further government action

Most people agree that racism is unacceptable. Racism can create violence and lead to riots and injury. In 1976 the British government passed the Race Relations Act. This made it illegal to discriminate against any person on the grounds of their race, colour, nationality, or ethnic or national origin, in terms of access to employment, housing, education or government social services. It also made it illegal for any person to stir up racial hatred through using or publishing abusive, insulting or threatening words in public. The Act aims to give equal rights for ethnic minorities and religions.

To enforce the Race Relations Act, the government set up the Commission for Racial Equality, also in 1976. It has three important duties:

- to fight against racial discrimination
- to make people understand the importance of giving everyone an equal opportunity
- to check on how the law is working, and tell the government how it could be improved.

The Commission is still active today, seeking to educate the public on the importance of racial equality. It deals with complaints of racism. The majority of its work involves investigating cases of bullying and racism at work, including people being denied the opportunity of promotion despite being the best qualified person for the job.

Activities

4 In 2005 the British government introduced a 'Britishness' test, which must be taken by any person wishing to become a UK resident. It tests a person's ability to read English and requires the candidate to have a basic knowledge of typical British life. However, the tests have been criticised for lacking perspective and many UK-born citizens would find the questions difficult. Questions have included:

- Where are Geordie, Cockney and Scouse dialects spoken?
- What is the Church of England and who is its head?
- What is the Queen's official role and what ceremonial duties does she have?
- Which of these courts uses a jury system?
  Magistrates' Court, Crown Court, Youth Court or *County Court.*

Can you answer all of these questions?

5 Explain why you think racial discrimination is still a problem in the UK.

6 Evaluate to what extent you think the government has been successful in combating racism.

Activities

7 What can you find out about new government initiatives such as:

- **Citizen Days** in all local areas in England. These will celebrate both national and local culture, and stress shared local tradition alongside shared British values such as respect for the rule of law, tolerance and democracy.
- **Information packs for new migrants**. These will set out guidelines on British cultural norms – including tolerance and understanding of other faiths and communities.

Despite government legislation and action there still exists a gap between minorities; nearly two-thirds of ethnic minorities live in the 88 poorest areas of the country. Of these, 74 per cent of all Asian-origin children in the UK live in poverty.

Summary

The UK is a country that is opposed to racism, and the government has passed laws to protect individuals and minority groups. Most people are able to see the benefits of community cohesion, although racism is still frequent. New investment has been given to communities to tackle these problems.

4.6 The work of the Roman Catholic Church to help asylum seekers and immigrant workers

Learning outcomes

By the end of this lesson you should be able to:

- understand why people seek refuge in the UK
- explore what motivates Christians to help people
- examine the ways the Roman Catholic Church helps asylum seekers.

Activities

1 What factors do you think would make a person leave behind everything they had to move to another country?

2 Discuss how you would find out if a person had really been forced to flee their country.

The influx of immigrants has changed dramatically over the last decade and migration has gone to the top of the public policy agenda. The newspapers and television report on workers entering the EU, and communities express fears that British citizens are losing jobs due to cheaper 'foreign' labour. Some people leave their homelands simply for a better standard of life and for greater opportunities, whereas others leave to escape torture, persecution, civil wars or environmental disasters. The latter are refugees and asylum seekers. Historically, Christians have always tried to help these groups when they come into a country.

Catholics know that they must continue the long Christian tradition of hospitality to strangers and immigrants in their community. The Roman Catholic Church believes that the reasons why people are seeking to leave their country, whether legally or as illegal immigrants, must always be kept in mind.

The Holy Family were uprooted several times from their community. First Mary and Joseph had to travel from Nazareth to Bethlehem for the census, then they had to flee to Egypt, and finally they returned to Galilee. The first people to worship and see Jesus were not his relatives but strangers (Matthew 2:7–16).

Why do they help?

'I was a stranger and you did not invite me in.' (Matthew 25:43)

In the Bible, Christians are told that it is essential to recall that all human beings, regardless of the labels given to them, are entitled to their human dignity and rights. In speaking out for the rights of immigrants, refugees and migrants, the Church is upholding the fundamental Christian belief that human beings are made in the image and likeness of God (Genesis 1:27).

The Catholic Church calls for its members not to view immigrants as mere objects, but as human beings created in the image of God.

'I tell you the truth, whatever you did for one of the least of these brothers of mine, you did for me.' (Matthew 25:40)

'Continue to love each other like brothers, and remember always to welcome strangers, for by doing this, some people have entertained angels without knowing it.' (Hebrews 13:1–2)

The Common Good and Catholic Social Teaching (1997) confirms this view in its statement: 'Christ taught us that our neighbour is universal, so loving our neighbour has global dimensions. Solidarity with our neighbour is also about the promotion of equality of rights and equality of opportunities; hence we must oppose all forms of discrimination and racism.'

How do they help?

The Catholic Church provides help for asylum seekers and refugees in many ways:

- **Education**: They educate people generally in the challenges and problems that immigrants to the UK might face. They also ensure that Christians are aware of the messages of the Gospel and seek to take this message into the community.
- **Prayer**: The Catholic Church prays for those people who are being persecuted at the hands of others and for all those who are forced to leave their families and communities.
- **Practical help**: Most parishes have a group called the SVP (St Vincent de Paul). The SVP offers practical help, support and advice for those who are in need. They may also provide help with low-cost housing, discount furniture and clothing, and some parishes offer assistance with reading and language difficulties.

Some areas are able to take their help a stage further. The Asylum Seekers and Refugees Project is an initiative of Hexham and Newcastle Catholic Diocese. It works to offer friendship and support to asylum seekers and refugees living in the diocese. The project has several weekly drop-in sessions staffed by volunteers in church premises and community centres. The volunteers help by making teas and coffees, chatting, joining in games (e.g. board games, pool, table tennis) and generally making people feel welcome.

Many parishes have responded to the recent immigration of Polish people and offer a weekly Mass in Polish.

Catholics help those seeking refuge in practical ways.

ResultsPlus
Build better answers

Explain why many Roman Catholics help asylum seekers and/or immigrant workers? (8 marks)

 Basic, 1–2-mark answers
Basic answers will just give one or two brief reasons without developing them or one developed reason.

 Good, 3–6-mark answers
Good answers (3–4 marks) will give up to four brief reasons; one developed and one brief reason; or two developed reasons. Better answers (5–6 marks) will give either three developed reasons, or a couple of developed reasons along with a couple of brief reasons.

 Excellent, 7–8-mark answers
Most excellent answers give four developed reasons. Answers that give two fully-developed reasons (which means lots of explanation!) will also reach 7–8 marks. All excellent answers will use some key terms and good English as this is taken into account on (c) questions.

Summary

The Catholic Church teaches that people must treat strangers with respect and remember that we are all made in the image of God. To support this, they offer help, prayers and advice to those seeking a home in the UK.

Activities

3   (a)   Who do you think Jesus meant when he talked about loving your neighbour?

(b)   Describe an example that Jesus gave about loving your neighbour.

(c)   Can you find any examples in your own community of people who have helped their 'neighbour'?

4.7 Why Roman Catholics should promote racial harmony

> ## Learning outcomes
>
> By the end of this lesson, you should be able to:
>
> - understand what racial harmony is
> - explain why Roman Catholics promote racial harmony.

The word 'catholic' means 'universal' or 'worldwide'. This could be used to summarise the Roman Catholic Church, as it has members from every country in the world and of every nationality.

Almost 30 per cent of the world's population is Catholic, and of this figure 70 per cent are non-white and non-European. The increase and greater freedom in travel has changed the demographics (population make-up) of many Catholic parishes. Many UK parishes now have Catholic members from other countries, such as India, the Philippines and Poland. When people come to a country to work, they may also wish to continue to worship. The Roman Catholic Church tries to help them do so.

The Catholic Church's ethnic diversity is also reflected in its leadership. It has cardinals and bishops from many different countries. They work in their home countries and at an international level, promoting Gospel values and unity between all faiths and races.

Jesus was brought up in a multi-ethnic and multi-cultural society. The Jews were a minority group in their own country, making up about 30 per cent of the total population. Jesus rejected the narrow exclusivity preached by religious groups and told the people that the Kingdom of God was open to all. Jesus taught that this kingdom would attract people from north and south, east and west. The Catholic Church believes that it should promote racial harmony because of Jesus's example.

> ## Activities
>
> 1 Discuss the features that suggest the Catholic Church is universal.
> 2 What are the benefits of having many different nationalities united in one belief?
> 3 Describe how a local church can welcome people who have just arrived in their parish from another country.

Jesus told his followers the story of the Good Samaritan (Luke 10:25–37). This parable talks about loving your neighbour, even if your neighbour is a stranger or an enemy. In this parable, Jesus makes clear that his followers should make no distinction between people who have different religions or who are from different countries. Those who refuse to love others – whatever their background, race or religion – cannot hope to be part of God's kingdom. Catholics believe that in order to be a follower of Jesus you must not reject anyone who is in need.

The Catholic Church has members from across the world – do you think this promotes racial understanding?

The Bible also gives examples of when Jesus treated people of a different race equally. He healed a servant belonging to a Roman soldier (Luke 4), and at the well he treated a Samaritan woman as his equal.

St Paul teaches in Galatians 3:26–28 that in God there are no more distinctions, and that everyone is equal in Christ.

All the Christian Churches have spoken about and issued statements condemning racism and asking their followers to work towards racial harmony. In 1998 the following statement was released to the press from Churches Together, an organisation that links the Churches.

'Respect for the humanity we share with each and every neighbour is the only basis for a peaceful and good society. Any attack on the dignity and human rights of any racial or religious group damages all of us.' (From the Churches Together letter to the press, May 1998)

Activities

4 Give an account of the biblical teachings that Roman Catholics might use in forming their views about racial harmony, and explain how these teachings are important in today's world. Use the writing frame below to help you:

Jesus lived in a multi-ethnic society, and his response was to ....

Jesus's example shows that he did not limit his teaching or his healing to just the Jews. His healing of the Roman officer's servant shows us that ....

Jesus also treated the Samaritan woman equally. This shows ....

Jesus's teaching in the Good Samaritan tells his followers that they should

....

St Paul explained ....

From this teaching we can see that Jesus wants his followers to ....

ResultsPlus
Build better answers

'If everyone were religious there would be no racism.'
In your answer you should refer to Roman Catholic Christianity.
(i) Do you agree? Give reasons for your opinion. (3 marks)
(ii) Give reasons why some people may disagree with you. (3 marks)

■ **Basic, 1-mark answers**
Basic answers to both parts of the question will give just one simple reason for their opinion and one simple reason for the opposite point of view.

● **Good, 2-mark answers**
Good answers will receive two marks for two simple reasons or one developed reason. Therefore if they do this for both their own opinion and the opposite point of view, they will get four marks in total. However, if the answer to both parts of the question does not include the Roman Catholic view, then students cannot get more than three marks in total.

▲ **Excellent, 3-mark answers**
Excellent answers will give three simple reasons, two developed reasons or one fully developed reason. If they do this for their own opinion and the opposite point of view they will get six marks in total.

Activities

Challenge
5 Explain why you think it is important that the Christian Churches work together.

Summary

Catholics are taught that racism is against the message of the Gospel. They are inspired by the Bible's teachings and the example of Jesus. They know that they have a responsibility to work for justice and fairness.

4.8 Differences in Christian attitudes to other religions

Learning outcomes

By the end of this lesson, you should be able to:

● describe the different Christian attitudes towards other religions

● understand why this range of attitudes exists.

edexcel ⠿ key terms

Religious freedom – The right to practise your religion and change your religion.

Religious pluralism – Accepting all religions as having an equal right to coexist.

Within a society such as the UK, which has **religious freedom**, there is a belief that everyone should be free to worship (or reject) whatever religion they choose without the risk of punishment or condemnation. However, some religious people are not so liberal and claim that only their religion is right and that everyone should follow it. The major Christian Churches agree that there should be no religious discrimination, but there are differences in the attitudes various groups of Christians hold towards other religions. There are three main approaches.

Exclusivism – Only those who believe in Jesus will be saved.

Inclusivism – Christianity has the whole truth, whereas other religions only have 'part of the truth' and therefore should be allowed to continue their search for God unhindered.

Pluralism – All faiths are equal and all are valid paths to God.

The Roman Catholic view

Catholics and many other Christians have an inclusivist view. They believe that people can come to God through different religious paths, but only Christianity has the full truth. They think that everyone has the right to follow or not follow any religion they wish, and that all religions must be

Activities

The landscape of Britain reflects its multi-faith society.

1 What does the illustration above tell us about UK society?

2 Why do you think it is important for people to be able to choose what religion they follow?

respected. Some of these may even get to Heaven. However, the Catholic Church believes that only Christianity is the one religion with the complete truth. While they should try to bring members of other faiths into Christianity, they must also accept that people can come to God in their own way.

They believe this because:

● the Bible teaches that the true nature of God was shown through Jesus Christ

● it is the teaching of the Catholic Church.

> 'Although in ways known only to himself God can lead those, who through no fault of their own, are ignorant of the Gospel, to that faith without which it is impossible to please him, the Church still has the obligation and also the sacred right to evangelise all men.' (Catechism of the Catholic Church, 848)

Exclusivist view

This view is often held by groups of evangelical Protestants and other traditional Christians. They believe that there is only one way to God – and that it is through Jesus. They believe that they have a duty and a responsibility to convert people to Christianity.

They think this because:

- Jesus said, '*I am the way and the truth and the life. No one comes to the Father except through me*' (John 14:6). They would also maintain that only Christians will go to Heaven.
- Jesus told his disciples, '*go to all peoples everywhere and make them my disciples; baptise them...*' (Matthew 28:19). This inspires believers to try to convert people to Christianity.
- The Bible says, '*Love your neighbour*'. Believers think that telling others about God is the most loving thing to do.

Activities

3   Do you think it is fair to convert people to Christianity? Give your reasons why and then give arguments against your opinion.

Pluralist view

This approach is a more liberal, modern approach than the previous two. Many liberal Christians believe in **religious pluralism**. They feel that it is not fair to try to convert people from other faiths. They believe that all the main religions, including Christianity, have produced both good and bad people. All religions are equal to one another. What suits one person will not necessarily suit another.

They believe this because:

- They look to the fact that Jesus said, '*In my Father's house there are many rooms*' (John 14:2). They believe that this means there is room in Heaven for different religions.
- The Roman soldier said, '*Truly this was the Son of God*' (Matthew 27:54). This is recognition of Jesus by a person of another faith.
- Jesus told the criminal on the cross that he would be in paradise with him.
- They believe God is out there waiting to be discovered and it is up to each individual to make that discovery for themselves. They are totally free to choose which path they take.

Activities

Challenge

4   Explain why there are different attitudes among Christians towards other religions.

5   Which view do you feel that you identify with? Give a speech on these reasons.

Summary

It is Christian teaching that people should not suffer from any form of religious discrimination. Exclusivism claims that the Christian religion is the only way to come to God. Inclusivism claims that other religions hold part of the truth but Christianity holds the full truth. Pluralism claims that there are many ways to find God.

4.9 The UK as a multi-faith society

Learning outcomes

By the end of this lesson you should be able to:

● understand and explain what a multi-faith society is

● detail some benefits of a multi-faith society

● describe some problems that a multi-faith society might face

● examine the evidence and evaluate your own opinion on a multi-faith society.

edexcel key terms

Interfaith marriages – Marriage where the husband and wife are from different religions.

Multi-faith society – Many different religions living together in one society.

The UK is a country made up of many different races, faiths, social groups and cultures. A **multi-faith society** has people of several different faiths and religious beliefs all living alongside each other in relative harmony. Such a society believes that everyone has the right to religious freedom, the freedom to worship freely in whatever religion they choose. They also accept that every religion has a right to coexist; this religious pluralism means that they do not view any religion as having the ultimate, exclusive truth.

From single faith to multi-faith

Before the Second World War few people in the UK followed a religion other than Christianity. Since then, immigrants have come from the West Indies, India, Pakistan, Bangladesh, Hong Kong, Tanzania, Uganda, Kenya and many other countries. This has led to a growth of significant communities of Hindus, Muslims and Sikhs in the UK. Religious communities and places of worship have gradually built up around them to support these believing groups.

Benefits of a multi-faith society

Positive aspects include:

● increased tolerance between people, building community cohesion

● a deeper understanding of different ways of life and traditional customs

● opportunities to gain knowledge and an understanding of another person's faith

● broader thinking through shared religious ideas

● strengthened faith, through seeing the example of other believers.

The sense of religious freedom and understanding that can exist in a multi-faith society can help to stop religious conflicts such as those between Protestant and Catholic Christians in Northern Ireland or between Hindus, Muslims and Sikhs in India.

Activities

1 **(a)** How many of the major world faiths can you name?

(b) Look at these symbols. Which faith does each represent? Draw them and write the world faith next to it.

However, a multi-faith Britain has not been easy to achieve. There still exists a great deal of religious tension in certain areas of the country. Some people feel that religious tolerance and freedom will lead to their own views being ignored and weakened. Some feel that Britain's heritage as a Christian country is being threatened.

Problems arising within a multi-faith society

Interfaith marriages

Within a multi-faith society, individuals may sometimes wish to marry people of a different faith. This can cause problems, as often believing parents want their offspring to marry within their own faith. The problems include:

- what type of religious wedding ceremony can they have?
- what religion might any children be brought up in?
- will different death rituals apply, e.g. will a couple be buried in different parts of a graveyard according to their religion?
- what religious community will they and their children belong to?

Most faiths will offer advice on how to create a successful **interfaith marriage**. The Roman Catholic Church also gives special permission for Catholics to marry people of another faith.

Activities

2 Outline the advantages of an interfaith marriage.

3 What 'problems' do you think might occur in a multi-faith society?

4 'No one has the right to tell people their religion is the best.' Do you agree? Explain your opinion.

Conversion

Some religions teach that their beliefs are the only right ones. Traditional Protestants, for example, feel that it is their duty to convert people to Christianity. They believe that all other religions are wrong and that they need to show people how Christianity holds the correct answers. This can be viewed as discrimination, as they appear to be saying their religion is superior to others.

Upbringing of children

Believing families living within a multi-faith society may still choose to bring their children up in their own faith and culture. This will involve teaching, prayer, encouraging the children in the customs of the faith and possibly specific faith schooling. This can sometimes cause misunderstanding, conflict and resentment in other parts of the community.

ResultsPlus
Build better answers

Explain why trying to convert people may cause problems in a multi-faith society. (8 marks)

■ **Basic, 1–2-mark answers**
Basic answers only focus on one reason or offer a variety of reasons without explaining them.

● **Good, 3–6-mark answers**
These answers will offer two or three developed reasons or may offer many reasons without explaining them.

▲ **Excellent, 7–8-mark answers**
The best answers will offer many reasons and develop at least two of them. The main reason that better answers will use is that conversion implies that one religion is better than another, which is against the idea of an equal multi-faith society. The candidate will use some key terms and good English.

Summary

The UK allows religious freedom so that individuals can worship in whatever religion they want. This freedom can help communities to understand each other and in turn helps to reduce racial tension. Problems that still arise include issues such as marriage, burial, conversion and upbringing.

4.10 Ways in which religions work to promote community cohesion in the UK

Learning outcomes

By the end of this lesson you should be able to:

● explain how religions promote community cohesion

● express your own opinion on how life has changed in the UK since it has become a multi-faith society.

Activities

1 Make a spider diagram of any values that you think different religions may have in common.

2 Discuss why you think they have these shared values.

Does religion teach people the same moral values?

Different religious faith groups do not usually want to live in conflict with each other. Acts of aggression and violence go against all faith beliefs. Nevertheless, in order to live together in harmony, faith groups need to work together to promote community cohesion, understanding and friendship. This can require a lot of hard work and effort. They need to:

● recognise all the things that their faith and cultures have in common
● respect the differences that arise between them
● listen to each other's views
● learn to accept and live and work in unity rather than in opposition to each other
● share common values such as respect, tolerance, charity and non-violence.

Building community cohesion through religious groups

Religions are united in a belief in a higher presence, something greater than ourselves. They also share the teaching that God created humankind to form and grow in a relationship with God. It is these beliefs that have allowed faiths to work together. Britain's oldest national inter-faith organisation is the Council of Christians and Jews. It works to promote religious and cultural understanding between Christians and Jews, aiming to eliminate religious and racial prejudice and discrimination, and to promote religious and racial harmony.

There are also other ecumenical organisations, such as Churches Together, which bring Christian Churches together in the unity of Christ.

Religions can also promote community cohesion through the celebration of festivals and worship. In Liverpool, Church leaders hold an inaugural service in Liverpool's two cathedrals and include a walk of witness along Hope Street, which links the two together. Members from all world faiths take part in the service. This serves to foster unity in worship, witness and practical action.

However, some people do not like this unity and several councils have banned shops from displaying Christmas decorations, instead asking them to display 'Seasons Greetings' in the belief that the explicitly Christian Christmas decorations may offend people of other faiths.

Does this unite or divide a community?

Activities

3   Why do you think some councils have banned the use of Christmas decorations?

4   Do you think this move will unite the community? Give reasons for your view and then try to counter-argue your opinion.

Community cohesion and faith schools

The Catholic Church believes that all humans should be treated equally and fairly. As a result, they promote community cohesion and provide support through parishes to communities. Community cohesion can also be supported through the existence of faith schools. These schools base their mission on religious values. The faith of the school should be evident in all aspects of the curriculum, through promoting a person's uniqueness, encouraging pupils on their journey in faith and be reflected in the school's policies and mission statement. In the UK there are 21,000 faith schools; the majority are Christian-based, with only 7 Islamic and 2 Sikh schools. The government has made a promise to support people who wish to establish faith schools as they believe they create understanding between faiths. However, many people are opposed to this move, claiming they are too exclusive in their teaching and do not expose pupils to other faiths and practices.

For discussion

'Faith schools should be made to teach all religions.' Discuss your opinions about this statement with the person next to you and then share them with your class.

Catholic Cardinal Tauran issued a greeting calling for Christians and Muslims to unite in upholding the dignity of the family. In his message, the Cardinal described the family as the 'fundamental cell of society', reminding us that the development of the human person and society as a whole depends on the healthiness of family life:

'How many people carry, sometimes for the whole of their life, the weight of the wounds of a difficult or dramatic family background? Christians and Muslims can and must work together to safeguard the dignity of the family, today and in the future.'

Cardinal Tauran

Activities

Challenge

5   Why do you think Cardinal Tauran felt he could appeal to both Muslims and Christians?

6   Describe how the two religions could work together on this task.

Summary

Religious groups in the UK work hard to establish unity among Christians and with world religions. At times problems arise, and this means that religious groups have to work together and listen to each other in order to resolve issues.

4.11 Presentation of issues on religion and community cohesion in the media

Learning outcomes

By the end of this lesson, you should be able to:

● describe how religious and community cohesion issues are dealt with by the media

● be able to give an example from television and radio that deals with community cohesion

● understand why it is important for the media to present issues correctly and in perspective.

Activities

1 Can you think of any other life or death situations in the media?

2 **(a)** Choose a favourite television programme. Think back over recent storylines and highlight for discussion all those that have religious or community cohesion situations.

(b) Select one of the storylines and explain how you think it was dealt with and if you think the programme makers could have dealt with the issue better.

How religion and community cohesion are presented in the media

It is now easier than ever to communicate our thoughts and ideas with others. We are able to see events that happen all over the world almost at the same time they are occurring.

Events of everyday life are also portrayed for people's entertainment. These range from fictional situations such as in soap operas or in films with actors to real-time events shown on reality television. Many of these situations include references to issues of religion or community cohesion.

Some examples are shown in the photos on this page.

The Simpsons – *shows how a family deals with issues such as Marge's Christian faith, and also shows a multi-faith society in action*

The Vicar of Dibley – *deals with the topic of women priests*

Coronation Street – *Todd's homosexuality.*

In addition to these, there are also documentary programmes that investigate and report on controversial and topical issues such as terrorism, abortion, euthanasia, genetics and other medical ethics. Two popular documentary programmes are *Everyman* and *Panorama*.

Radio broadcasts also often deal with issues such as sex, sexuality and race relations.

Religious programmes, such as *Songs of Praise*, describe events in the lives of believers and work in parishes, as well as dealing with issues of conversion and community outreach.

Advertising and racism

According to an Independent Television Commission report, the use of stereotypes in television advertisements can reinforce racism and school bullying. Black and ethnic minority respondents said they felt advertising did not reflect the UK's cultural diversity, and some commercials were overtly racist. An advert for a tea company was criticised by many Asian people who were surveyed for portraying workers on a tea plantation in a patronising and offensive way. The report also highlighted commercials showing children who were overweight or wearing glasses, as this could exacerbate school bullying. On the other hand, an advert for a curry sauce was praised for featuring British Asians with strong Glaswegian accents.

Are the media fair?

A major problem faced by all forms of media coverage on religious and community cohesion issues is the ability to remain unbiased. In 2006, Britain's most senior police commissioner, Sir Ian Blair, accused the media of 'institutional racism' over its reporting of murders. He said 'murders in minority communities appeared "not to interest the mainstream media", while middle-class, white victims attracted much more coverage'. This supports other claims made that news broadcasters only show one side of an event and often cover extreme elements of a story that do not give the viewer a full understanding of the event.

YOU WRITE WHAT YOU'RE TOLD!

THANKS, CORPORATE NEWS!
We Couldn't Control The People Without You
A MESSAGE FROM THE MINISTRY OF HOMELAND SECURITY

Summary

• Many non-religious broadcasts deal with religious and community issues from a secular viewpoint and sometimes from a religious viewpoint.

• Some broadcasts can be seen as stereotypical in their choice of characters. Some critics believe that television news is not always fair in its reporting.

examzone

Know Zone
Religion and community cohesion

Quick quiz

1 Give an example of 'discrimination'.

2 What is meant by 'community cohesion'?

3 How have attitudes towards gender roles in the UK changed in recent years?

4 Explain two different Christian attitudes towards women in the ministry.

5 Give an example of how the government has tried to promote community cohesion.

6 Explain what makes up a multi-faith society.

7 Recall two Gospel stories that inspire Christians to promote racial harmony.

8 Explain three different Christian attitudes towards other religions.

9 What are the advantages and disadvantages of living in a multi-faith society?

10 How have religious and community issues been highlighted in television soaps?

Plenary activity

Create your own soap opera; in your drama you will need to tackle discrimination.

In one scene you will have two characters, one male and one female and one white, one not. Both are in their twenties. The man is a Muslim and the woman is a Christian. They have fallen in love and decide to get married in the UK. Using some or all of the sections in this unit, write a short report about the issues each of them faces prior to the marriage and consider how these difficulties might be overcome.

Consider how the Christian woman feels and consider the questions she must ask herself. Try to get into the minds of these characters so that what they feel is real to you and to someone who might read your report. Try to get deeply into the reasons why they believe and act as they do.

Find in your community or school two people from very different social or ethnic backgrounds and interview them, and then write a short account of their vision for the future and their view of what society is like. Compare the two views and discuss whether both people feel that the country they live in is equal.

Find out more

A good way to find out more is to visit your local community centre, college or library and find out what multi-faith or multi-ethnic events are taking place in your area. Many churches also hold community events. Take the opportunity to pick up leaflets that will tell you what is going on and what it is all about. You could even organise a visit to a place of worship – remember to call beforehand so that they can give you some instructions, e.g. if you need to remove your shoes. Ask your teacher if he or she can arrange for members of other religious or community groups to visit your school.

Student tips

When I studied these topics for my GCSE I made sure that I knew all the significant facts and understood all the main arguments for and against controversial issues. In this way, I could be sure of getting full marks for all the questions that asked for knowledge and understanding. For example, I could use my knowledge and understanding of the issues that cause racial tension to answer questions on the causes and possible solutions to such problems.

Self-evaluation checklist

How well have you understood the topics in this section? In the first column of the table below use the following code to rate your understanding:

Green – I understand this fully

Orange – I am confident I can answer most questions on this

Red – I need to do a lot more work on this topic.

In the second and third columns you need to think about:

- Whether you have an opinion on this topic and could give reasons for that opinion if asked
- Whether you can give the opinion of someone who disagrees with you and give reasons for this alternative opinion.

Content covered	My understanding is red/orange/green	Can I give my opinion?	Can I give an alternative opinion?
How attitudes have changed towards gender roles in the UK			
The different Christian attitudes to equal rights for women in religion			
How the UK works as a multi-ethnic society			
The benefits and problems of a multi-ethnic society			
The current legislation and the actions of the government to prevent racism			
How the Catholic Church helps asylum seekers and refugees in the UK			
Why Catholics feel they should help promote racial harmony			
The different Christian attitudes to other religions (exclusivism, inclusivism, pluralism)			
The issues that are raised for religion by a multi-faith society, interfaith marriage, and conversion			
Government laws to prevent racism and promote racial harmony			
The ways in which religions work to promote community cohesion in the UK			
Problems caused through racial and multi-faith unrest			
How religion and the community has been portrayed in the media			
Problems with media presentation of controversial issues			
How programmes may influence people's views about religion and community cohesion.			

Know Zone
Religion and community cohesion

Introduction

In the exam you will see a choice of two questions on this module. Each question will include four tasks, which test your knowledge, understanding and evaluation of the material covered. A 2-mark question will ask you to define a term; a 4-mark question will ask your opinion on a point of view; an 8-mark question will ask you to explain a particular belief or idea; a 6-mark question will ask for your opinion on a point of view and ask you to consider an alternative point of view.

You must give your opinion, but make sure you do give two clear and thought-out reasons. These can be ones you have learned in class, even if they are not your own opinion. You mustn't use terms such as 'rubbish' or 'useless' as these don't show that you are able to think things through carefully.

Mini exam paper

(a) What is a **multi-ethnic society?** (2 marks)

(b) Do you think women should have equal rights in religion?

Give **two** reasons for your point of view. (4 marks)

(c) Explain why interfaith marriages may cause problems for religious families. (8 marks)

(d) 'If everyone were religious there would be no racism.' In your answer you should refer to Roman Catholic Christianity.

(i) Do you agree? Give reasons for your opinion. (3 marks)

(ii) Give reasons why some people may disagree with you. (3 marks)

Just give a short, accurate definition.

The word 'explain' means you should give examples of the problems that religious families may have to deal with when faced with the issue of an interfaith marriage. Remember that you are writing about the problems of a religious family, and so these problems will be of a religious nature. Don't just list problems – explain why they are problems. This question is worth 8 marks so spend a longer amount of time on it. You will also be assessed on your use of language in this question.

Don't make things up – use reasons you have learned in class. Don't forget to refer to Roman Catholic Christianity.

Now you must to give the opposite point of view. As before, give reasons you have learned in class. You must show you understand why people have these other views, even if you don't agree with them.

Mark scheme

(a) will earn you **2 marks** for a correct answer, and **1 mark** for a partially correct answer.

(b) To earn up to the full **4 marks** you need to give two reasons and to develop them fully. Two brief reasons or only one developed reason will earn **2 marks**.

(c) You can earn **7–8 marks** by giving up to four reasons, but the fewer reasons you give, the more you must develop them. Because you are being assessed on use of language, you also need to take care to express your understanding in a clear style of English, and make some use of specialist vocabulary.

(d) To go beyond **3 marks** for the whole of this question you must refer to Roman Catholicism. The more you are able to develop your reasons, the more marks you will earn. Three simple reasons can earn you the same mark as one fully developed reason.

ResultsPlus
Maximise your marks

(c) Explain why interfaith marriages may cause problems for religious families. (8 marks)

Student answer	Examiner comments	Improved student answer
Interfaith marriages cause problems to religious families because the family may feel that their religion is right and the other religion is wrong.	The candidate has given a reason, but this has not been developed fully.	Interfaith marriages may cause problems for religious families because members will have different beliefs and values. For example, the couple will need to agree on how to bring up their children, and what religion their children will belong to. There could be controversy over key issues such as homosexuality and arranged marriages.
Also, they may feel that if their son or daughter is getting married, that they will have to change their religious faith and join a religion whose teachings they do not believe in.	Again, a good reason is given but this is not developed.	If one of the two people getting married decides to practise a different religion to suit their partner's family, this might cause worry and concern. For example, family members might worry that practising a religion that they haven't grown up with would be against the will of God, if the belief is not genuine.
Finally, the couple may not be able to have a religious wedding because of their different faiths and this means the family will not be able to celebrate the wedding properly.	This is another good reason that has not been developed. This answer will gain 4 marks because the candidate has given some correct reasons, but they have not really developed their answer.	The couple may not be able to have a religious wedding because of their different faiths and this means the family will not be able to celebrate the union according to the traditions they believe in. Also, if a Muslim and Christian marry, for example, the Christian side of the family may worry about whether they should give Christmas gifts or not, and both sides could worry about how to deal with religious festivals.

Welcome to exam zone

Revising for your exams can be a daunting prospect. In this part of the book we'll take you through the best way of revising for your exams, step by step, to ensure you get the best results possible.

Zone In!

Have you ever become so absorbed in a task that suddenly it feels entirely natural and easy to perform? This is a feeling familiar to many athletes and performers. They work hard to recreate it in competition in order to do their very best. It's a feeling of being 'in the zone', and if you can achieve that same feeling in an examination, the chances are you'll perform brilliantly.

The good news is that you can get 'in the zone' by taking some simple steps in advance of the exam. Here are our top tips.

UNDERSTAND IT

Make sure you understand the exam process and what revision you need to do. This will give you confidence and also help you to get things into proportion. These pages are a good place to find some starting pointers for performing well in exams.

FRIENDS AND FAMILY

Make sure that your friends and family know when you want to revise. Even share your revision plan with them. Learn to control your times with them, so you don't get distracted. This means you can have better quality time with them when you aren't revising, because you aren't worrying about what you ought to be doing.

DEAL WITH DISTRACTIONS

Think about the issues in your life that may interfere with revision. Write them all down. Then think about how you can deal with each so they don't affect your revision.

COMPARTMENTALISE

You might not be able to deal with all the issues that can distract you. For example, you may be worried about a friend who is ill, or just be afraid of the exam. In this case, there is still a useful technique you can use. Put all of these worries into an imagined box in your mind at the start of your revision (or in the exam) and mentally lock it. Only open it again at the end of your revision session (or exam).

DIET AND EXERCISE

Make sure you eat sensibly and exercise as well! If your body is not in the right state, how can your mind be? A substantial breakfast will set you up for the day, and a light evening meal will keep your energy levels high.

BUILD CONFIDENCE

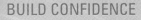

Use your revision time not only to revise content, but also to build your confidence in readiness for tackling the examination. For example, try tackling a short sequence of easy tasks in record time.

Planning Zone

The key to success in exams and revision often lies in good planning. Knowing **what** you need to do and **when** you need to do it is your best path to a stress-free experience. Here are some top tips in creating a great personal revision plan.

First of all, know your strengths and weaknesses.

Go through each topic making a list of how well you think you know the topic. Use your mock examination results and/or any other test results that are available as a check on your self-assessment. This will help you to plan your personal revision effectively, putting extra time into your weaker areas.

Next, create your plan!

Remember to make time for considering how topics interrelate.

For example, in PE you will be expected to know not just about the various muscles, but how these relate to various body types.

The specification quite clearly states when you are expected to be able to link one topic to another so plan this into your revision sessions.

You will be tested on this in the exam and you can gain valuable marks by showing your ability to do this.

Finally, follow the plan!

You can use the revision sections in the following pages to kick-start your revision.

113

MAY

SUNDAY	MONDAY	TUES

Be realistic about how much time you can devote to your revision, but also make sure you put in enough time. Give yourself regular breaks or different activities to give your life some variance. Revision need not be a prison sentence!

30

Find out your exam dates. Go to the Edexcel website **www.edexcel.com** to find all final exam dates, and check with your teacher.

1

view Secti
complete t
ractice ex
question

7

Chunk your revision in each subject down into smaller sections. This will make it more manageable and less daunting.

8

Draw up a list of all the dates from the start of your revision right through to your exams.

13

Review Sectio
Complete three
practice exam

20

Review Sectio
Try the Keywo
Quiz again

Make sure you allow time for assessing your progress against your initial self-assessment. Measuring progress will allow you to see and be encouraged by your improvement. These little victories will build your confidence.

22

EXAM DAY!

27

28

29

In this section, you need to show the examiner that you can understand the issues relating to belief in God (AO1) and that you can give your own point of view using reasons and evidence (AO2); you must also be able to give an alternative point of view and explain the reasons someone might think this.

The first step will be to learn the information. For this section it is things that cause people to believe in God and things that make people reject belief in God. You then must be able to explain how Christians (especially Roman Catholics) respond to the arguments for not believing in God – in particular their response to unanswered prayers, scientific explanations of the origins of the universe, and evil and suffering.

As part of the AO2 assessment you also have to be able to explain your own views, giving your reasons and evidence. You may find you agree with Roman Catholics or with the alternative arguments presented; you must be able to explain why. However, you must in the (d) questions be able to show that you understand that it is possible to have an alternative point of view from your own. You will be asked to give the reasons for this point of view.

Revision

Look back at the KnowZone at the end of the section on page 24. Complete the Self-evaluation checklist and think about areas you are stronger or weaker in, so that you can focus on those areas you are less confident about. You might like to try the Quick quiz or the Plenary activity at the end of the section, or the Support activity below. When you are ready for some exam practice, read through the KnowZone on pages 26–27. Then you could attempt the practice exam questions on this page.

Support activity

You will need to revise examples of two programmes about religions, in case a question on the media comes up in this section. As part of your revision, watch the programmes again. Jot down some notes either while you are watching or just after. You may like to consider these quotes and whether the programme supports or does not support the views:

- 'Religious programmes on television are usually supportive of religious believers.'
- 'Religious programmes on television say more about reasons not to believe in God than to believe in him.'
- 'Television programmes about religious beliefs discourage people from believing in God.'

Practice exam questions

(a) What is meant by **numinous**? (2 marks)

(b) Do you think God is the cause of the universe?

Give **two** reasons for your point of view. (4 marks)

(c) Explain how Roman Catholics respond to the problem of evil and suffering. (8 marks)

(d) 'Religious programmes on television or the radio encourage you to believe in God.' In your answer you should refer to Roman Catholic Christianity.

(i) Do you agree? Give reasons for your opinion. (3 marks)

(ii) Give reasons why some people may disagree with you. (3 marks)

The material in this section tends to deal a lot more with issues that are not just of concern to Roman Catholics, but to everyone. We all care about matters of life and death because we will all die but, until we do, we want to be sure that our life and the lives of others, whether they are close to us or not, are treated with respect.

It is important in this section that you ensure you gain marks from considering the particular concerns of Roman Catholics – concerns that might be quite different from your own but that may also be shared by some non-religious believers.

Make sure you understand what it is that makes these views distinctive for Roman Catholics – issues such as the sanctity of life and the belief that God created human beings for a special purpose. For example, a Catholic may say this is the reason they are against euthanasia; however a non-religious person may also be against euthanasia, because they think it is more important to preserve life than to take it away.

In this section it is also important to identify and understand why Catholic Christians have different attitudes to these issues.

Revision

Look back at the KnowZone at the end of the section on page 52. Read through the Self-evaluation chart and think about which your stronger and weaker areas are, so that you can focus on those areas you are less confident about. You might like to try the Quick Quiz or the Plenary activity at the end of the section, or the Support activity below. When you are ready for some exam practice, read through the KnowZone on pages 54–55. Then you could attempt the practice exam questions on this page.

Support activity

Question (d), about the paranormal is probably one of the trickier questions you could get, as it really is a matter of opinion, since no one can actually *prove* whether paranormal activity is genuine or not.

Your understanding of this area would be helped by finding out, as a class or in small groups, about some popular views on the paranormal. Find out about TV shows and so called 'celebrity' mediums, for example Tony Stockwell. They have an enormous following. Discuss why you think this is the case, and if there is anything that proves they are genuinely in touch with the paranormal.

Practice exam questions

(a) What is **resurrection**? (2 marks)

(b) Do you think we should help to relieve world poverty?

Give **two** reasons for your point of view. (4 marks)

(c) Choose **one** issue from Matters of life and death which has been presented in **one** form of the media, and say whether the treatment was fair to religious beliefs. (8 marks)

(d) 'The paranormal proves that there is life after death.' In your answer you should refer to Roman Catholic Christianity.

   (i) Do you agree? Give reasons for your opinion. (3 marks)

   (ii) Give reasons why some people may disagree with you. (3 marks)

In this section you are presented with issues to which different groups of Christians have different attitudes. It is important to learn and understand where these different attitudes come from and to appreciate that not all Christians believe the same thing. In this section you will also have to address some more controversial issues that you have not thought of before. Take your time to think about your attitude towards them and why you hold that. It is also acceptable to say you do not know what you think yet, as long as you have considered all the different points of view.

Revision

Look back at the KnowZone at the end of the section on page 80. Read through the self-evaluation chart and think about which are your stronger and weaker areas, so that you can focus on those areas you are less confident about. You might like to try the Quick Quiz or the Plenary activity at the end of the section, or the Support activity below. When you are ready for some exam practice, read through the KnowZone on pages 82–83. Then you could attempt the practice exam questions on this page.

Support activity

Question (b) on contraception (opposite) asks for your opinion without specifying that you refer to religion. It is a question that need not have anything to do with religion, but at the same time you need to make sure you show that you do understand religious views and that they might be held for special reasons. As a group or in pairs compare the attitudes towards contraception from the different Christian groups.

What do you think about the questions now, 'When does life begin?' and 'Is it ever right to kill?'. How might these questions be used in an argument about contraception? Do you agree with the use of contraception? Give reasons for your answer.

Practice exam questions

(a) What is **re-marriage**? (2 marks)

(b) Do you think it is right to use contraception?

Give **two** reasons for your point of view. (4 marks)

(c) Explain why some Christians allow divorce and some do not. (8 marks)

(d) 'Family life is more important for religious people than for non-religious people.'

In your answer you should refer to Roman Catholic Christianity.

   (i) Do you agree? Give reasons for your opinion. (3 marks)

   (ii) Give reasons why some people may disagree with you. (3 marks)